What it's like to be me

Written and illustrated entirely by disabled children

Edited by Helen Exley

FRIENDSHIP PRESS • NEW YORK

My thanks go to Emma, Jason, Tracey, Sharon, Julie, Stephen Old, Gavin, Stephen Rolt and Nick. They all go to Hangers Wood School in my home town of Watford. They are not only special people to know — but their insight, sense of fun and their attitude towards sometimes severe problems, have helped me a great deal in the preparation of this book.

This edition published 1984 by
Friendship Press, Inc.
Editorial Office: 475 Riverside Drive,
Room 772, New York, NY 10115
Distribution Office: P.O. Box 37844,
Cincinnati, OH 45237
© 1981 Exley Publications Ltd
ISBN 0-377-00144-9

Cover by Hyun Sun Ahn

Printed in Hungary by Kossuth Printing House, Budapest

To my special mother. With her courage, crazy sense of humour and love of life, she has turned the adversity and pain of two very badly behaved legs into a minor nuisance — and an endless source of funny stories for her family and friends.

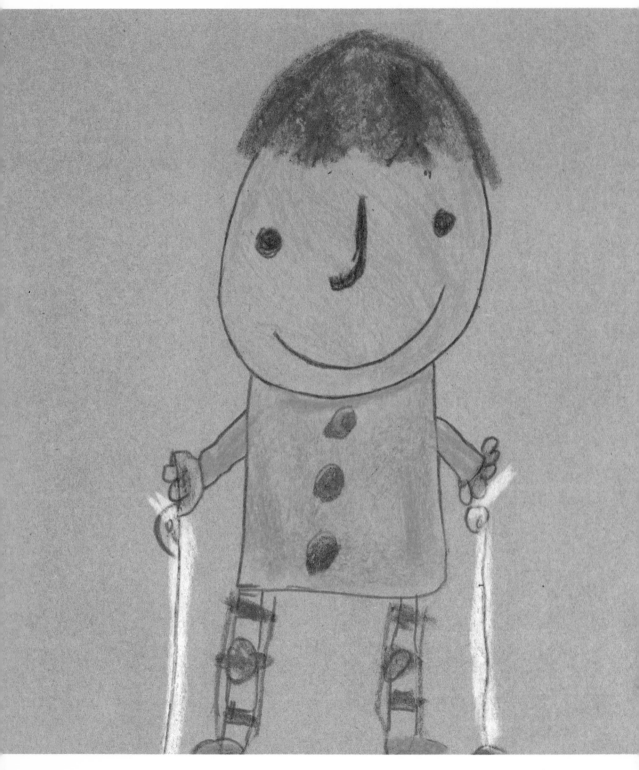

4

Alan Jones, 11

Introduction

'What it's like to be me' was prepared during the International Year of Disabled People as a contribution by disabled children themselves. The basic idea was that this was to be their book, entirely their own words, entirely their own drawings, saying what disabled children themselves really felt. I hope that the book will communicate strongly to other children, to parents, to teachers, and to all of us.

When I started the book, I suppose I expected it to be in some way miserable or depressing. But I found it the most genuinely happy book I have ever edited. I had several disabled friends in childhood and so I never had some of the usual prejudices about disabled people. Then I trained as a speech and deaf therapist and it never occurred to me that I had any prejudices left. But I presumably had this one lingering prejudice that disabled people were in some way unhappier than the rest of us. Editing the book has, in fact, been quite a profound experience for me. Sometimes you can go through years of work without feeling that what you have done has changed you or given you a different dimension. But in this case the book has changed my outlook on life. Suddenly all my problems seemed to shrink and I knew somewhere deep inside that whatever life threw at me from now on I'd have the strength, like the children had the strength, to face the future. Editing the book also happened to coincide with a serious illness in my own life, and as I faced my own fears, I could only be grateful to the children for being themselves, and saying the things they did. The book is such an overwhelming YES to life that I can only thank everyone involved: the children, the teachers, the parents and all those who helped so generously in spirit. The attitude behind all the entries — even the angry ones — was 'If I can do anything to help other kids understand, I will'. This comes through in the level of honesty in the writing. Even the critical comments are not destructive; they all attempt to communicate. To me, it is a real YES to life when a child who can only move one toe has bothered to speak out, not to get help for themselves but to make ordinary people understand.

The point that emerged again and again is that disabled people don't want your pity or 'kindness'. They want you to stay around, to be an ordinary friend. After all, they forget they are disabled: lots of entries for the book completely forgot to mention the fact. When asked to write about 'What it's like to be me' many of the children told me how they had spent the day, or how they enjoyed music or sport. The last thing they were concerned with was the fact that they may have taken an hour or more getting dressed. That sort of thing — a straightforward physical disability — is just part of life. They accept it. And they just want you to do the same.

Helen Exley

Why me?

A question that most disabled people ask themselves is "Why me?" Why, out of all the hundreds and thousands and millions of people it could have happened to, Why me? It's one question that there is no answer to.

Heather Jones

You're disabled and that's all there is to it. If you can't use your legs then there is no answer to it. I think people in chairs get jealous of a walking person! Take Stephen, for instance. *Why is it that he can walk and I can't?* Another thing is the operations. I have had about thirty-two operations, most on my back and I'm only thirteen.

Shaun Foulkes, 13

Although I have had a happy and enjoyable life so far, there have been times when I have sat in a room on my own and cried for no particular reason. It was a feeling of frustration more than anything. I sometimes ask myself the questions, "Why me? Why did it have to be me?" Of course, there is simply no answer to this question.

Tracey Lucas, 16

Klara Roseová ▶

◀ *Jin-Kyu Kim, 7*

8

Joys I'll never know

I will never know the joys of seeing colourful flowers and the blooming apple trees in spring. I will never know of the excitement of a ball game or watching a circus. I will never know how it is at a disco with flashing lights or the lights of the city at night. I will never know how it is watching Scotty, my guide dog, playing in the fields nor will I ever know the sight of the roaring Niagara Falls with my family. These are some of the joys I will never know.

Jean-Guy Forgeron, 10

I would like people to know that "What you've never had you don't miss" is not true. I do miss not being able to ride a bike or skateboard. I also miss not being able to do little things like splashing in rain puddles or being able to ride on a double decker bus. I would like them to understand what it is like to have to spend a large part of your childhood in hospital, but I would not wish it upon them.

Heather Jones

I can answer for myself

When I go out somewhere people ask my mother do I have sugar in my tea. It makes me feel as if I was a dummy.

Matthew Whiting

When I am out shopping with my Mom and we meet an Auntie or an old friend they never ask me how I am, they always ask my Mom. Most of the time I won't say anything, but sometimes I will sarcastically turn round and say "fine thanks, how are you?" Then they give me a funny look as if to say, "It speaks!"

Jacqueline Reed, 16

"Is she handicapped?"
We wanted somewhere to have lunch and mom noticed a children's park.
We went in. We sat down, while my brothers went off to play.
Just then a young girl came up to mom and said "Is she handicapped?" Mom said "Yes she can't use her legs properly."
"Will she kick me?"
"No of course not" I said.
The girl was astonished that I could speak for myself. Mom pulled down my sock to show her that my legs were just the same as hers. Gradually she realised that I was actually human. She pushed me round the park and introduced me to all her friends. I could tell she was enjoying herself. I was glad she came up to talk to me.

Celia Janney, 16

Does she want red jeans?
Laila Eide

11

Don't stare

Sometimes when I go out with my parents into town people on the streets look at me, for they have never seen a handicapped person. You would think that we were animals who had escaped from the zoo.

Denis Robineau, 14

I think I should wear a badge saying "Why waste good sight on me?" or something of that nature. I wonder if that would do the trick?

Helen Bryant, 12

People's attitude towards someone in a wheelchair can be very annoying and upsetting. Shopping on a Saturday can become a nightmare. People stand and stare at me or they give me funny looks. People never talk to you they talk to whoever is pushing you. People think that just because you can't walk, you can't talk either. I don't know why they think this but they do and it is very annoying. I would like to be treated normally like everyone else and one of my ambitions is to be able to go from one end of the street to the other without one person turning around to look at me. *Heather Jones*

Adults should be able to explain to their children that we are not able to walk and that's why we have to sit in a wheelchair. Then the children would not look at the handicapped peoples like at 'Martians'.

Monja Siegenthaler, 12 and Christine Bürki, 13

I wonder why people who look at a cripple react as if they had never seen such an invalid, though it is a frequent sight and this is painful for the person. If I see such a reaction at my appearance I feel like an animal in a cage.

Danuta Gieraltowska, 16

My name is Margaret Clark. I am in a wheelchair due to a handicap called spina-bifida. When I go to shopping malls and on outings people stare. I may be in a wheelchair but I'm just like normal people. I get hurt like other people do, I laugh like other people do. And I get angry like other people do.

Margaret Clark, 16

Neil Creaser, 10 ▶

its sad to be me when I go shopping

With my mun people look at me
but I look at then.

I feel the same as you

I am the same as you in that I can hear, learn and reason out things like you. I breath like you, I feel hungry like you and I have needs and wishes like you.

I'm different from you in that my limbs are not as strong as yours and I am not able to do some of the manual work which you are able to do.

I didn't like to be a disabled so it is so bitter in my heart. I would like to be taken care of. I would like to be loved. I would like to be respected and trusted. I would like to be considered too.

Mwaniki Makau, 10

Please treat us the same as you treat normal children for we're not like zombies: we're living human-beings and our brains function just the same as yours. *Laura Quinn, 16*

Although I am handicapped, I feel like a normal person. This is evidently not very clear to the vast majority of the general public. In fact, apart from being unable to walk, I am normal. Thank goodness all my friends (Yes, we do have them you know, we're quite sociable really!), have got this detail quite straight. Otherwise I would be a very lonely and unhappy person. In fact, I think that it is mainly due to them that I have been able to maintain my sanity.
There are quite a few people about, who go out in wheelchairs, so by now I would have thought that the general public would have become used to the idea, and not keep staring at us all the time. It is as though we are zombies. They make remarks like "Ooh mommy, look at that man" or "Mommy, why is that lady in a wheelchair?" Isn't it obvious, even to a person with the smallest amount of common sense? *Brian Wilson, 17*

But what is normality? Is there anyone in the vast world who can honestly say that they are perfect? All of us possess some sort of disorder. So this is my advice to those who are guilty of condemning handicapped people: take a look at yourselves first before you criticise. *Velma Sylvan, 16*

There are many things that I'd like all able-bodied children to understand. I would like them to know that just because there is something wrong with my spine it does not mean that my brain is affected. I wish that they would understand that being in a wheelchair does not make me any different from them. *Heather Jones*

My message to other children is: don't laugh at me but to thank your creator for what you are. Understand that I have a name, and blood like you. Please, why not be careful with me and understand my problem is not of my choosing. *Mutinda Kimilu, 9*

◀ *Dorota Lapińska*

*P. S Remember
I M
Normall*

James Hanoski

15

Que dois-je faire, m'en aller en pleurant,
répondre ou rester me faire insulter?

"What should I do? Go away crying, reply or stay to be insulted?"

Pierre Lacroix, 13

Please don't tease me

All the children look at me and say: look at that ugly little boy with a hump. That annoys me and makes me sad. Just because I have a hunchback it does not mean that my ears don't hear and my heart doesn't ache.

Jean Martin, 11

Since I was born, I have never been able to understand why I am not like the others. My handicap was not my fault, was it?

I was depressed because nobody played with me. They always jeered at me. When my brother took me to the park, I sat and saw them play with happiness. But why couldn't I play like them? I was lonely. Nobody played with me. But why did they always make a joke of me, and jeer and laugh at me? I just wanted to play with them very much, so I offered myself to be a horse so that they could ride on me. Everybody rode on me and enjoyed it, and I enjoyed it too.

Day after day I wanted to walk. Once I thought I could walk but when I tried I fell. And I thought that if they could get up and get down the stairs, why couldn't I. So I tried. I fell and my head was injured. My father asked me why I did it. I said I wanted to walk. My father looked so sad and told me I must wait.

From that day my father made me braces. I never had to crawl again. I was very glad that I could stand like the others. I loved it and thought that braces were my buddy. But even if I had braces someone still called me "four legs". I wanted to hit these faces but I couldn't. *Chalong Theppanmeong*

School, that is another thing altogether, some people treat you as a normal person but there are some people who think that it is a lot of fun to kick your walking stick out from under you or to accidentally-on-purpose push you over or do a very good job of getting you upset by teasing and name-calling.

Janette Cordery, 14

I don't like it when some people say: "What a squinty!" or "Bulging glasses" or "Blind mouse". *Margaret Pacak, 10*

The disabled should not be laughed at as if they are aliens from space.

Douglas Roper

Some of the kids who called me names didn't know what they were talking about. They were trying to be smart around their friends. They were being ignorant. Trying to think they were smart and they weren't. They were just being stupid. *Bobby Austin, 16*

Why do they scorn me?

Most of the problems that have confronted me have not been to do with my sight but have been caused by those who recognise my disability and scorn me for it.

Velma Sylvan, 16

When I was a little girl of about seven I moved to a new house and I was frightened to talk to other children because I was so scared because I can't talk very well. I was so upset.
One day I was playing with roller skates around the block and the boys and girls who could hear kept looking at me. I couldn't understand what they were talking about and they were teasing me about being deaf and dumb. When I went back to the house I started to cry. My Mom said "What's the problem." I said, "I've no friends to play with and they are teasing me. I don't understand what's wrong with them." My Mom explained to me, but I couldn't believe her. I wanted to make friends with them.

Mary Sallon, 13

I like the time of my life, but people hit me and I don't like being hit and I can't hit people back. I can't hit people like Paul because he's a bit tough for me. He hits me in school sometimes and my friends hit me at home, sometimes but not always.

Nigel Kay, 16

Some people shake their heads, look at my handicap or talk when I am not hearing. They even whisper to each other, they look at the way I walk. Others spit, some others laugh even as they give me an orange. They pray for me and nothing happens and all this makes me very sad. Helping me or any other handicapped child please remember not to make the above mistakes which I personally have tipped you.

Mutinda Kimilu, 9

My name is Suhil. I am a bit weak. I go to a school for physically handicapped children. I cannot hold a pencil properly. Some people call me spastic and handicapped twit. When they call me that I feel hurt but I don't say nothing because I feel scared. Sometimes my friend calls me names and hits me.

Suhil

Some people
Kick me with boots and it hurts me
people nuck a bout with my go cact . and
I hit them on the head

Neil Creaser

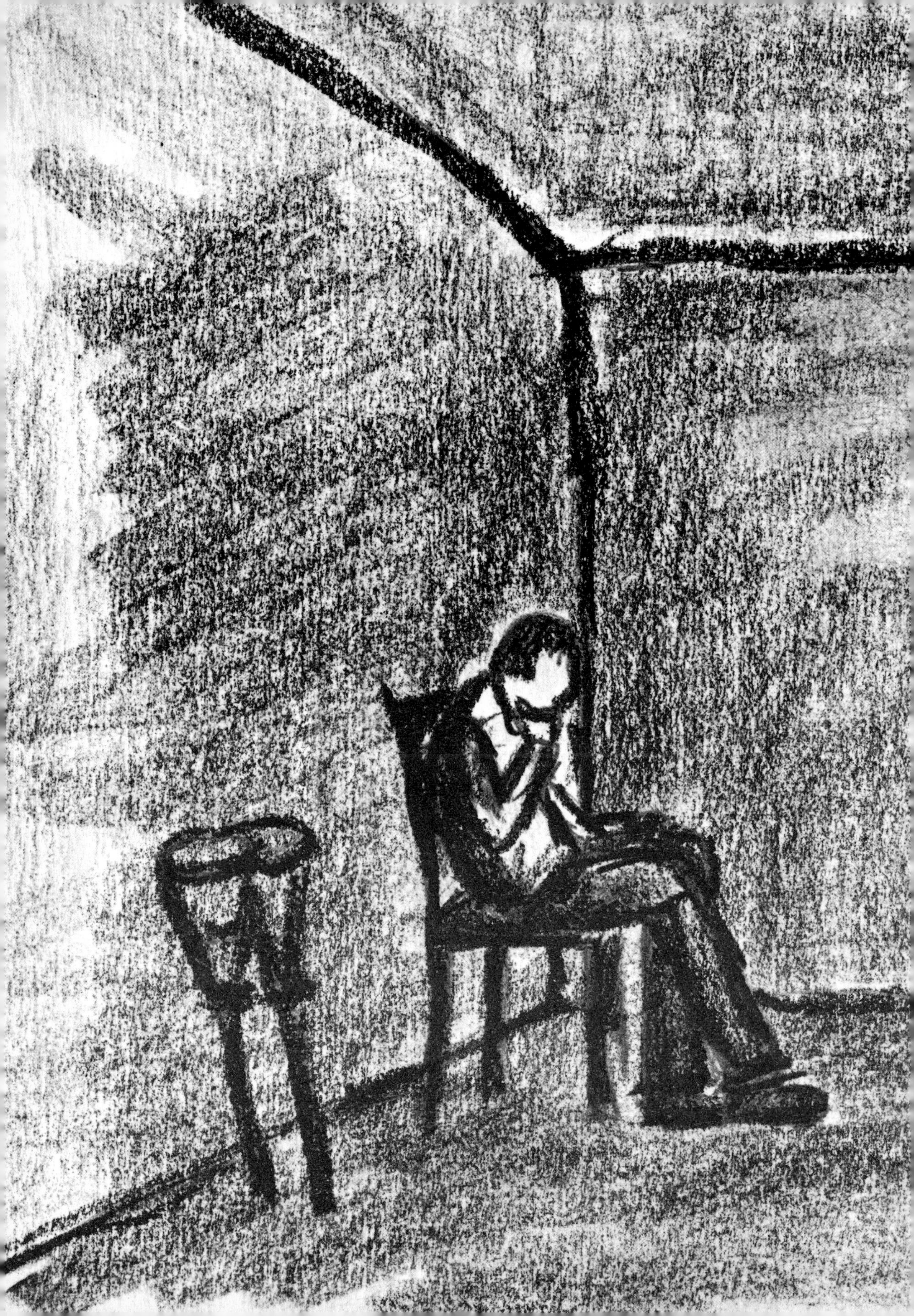

I am alone...

I am alone in this world.
I am lonely. All handicappeds are lonely.
I often feel lonely.
Left alone by everybody.

Silvio, 15

Maria Morkowska

I don't like it!

Do you sometimes find life hard? Then imagine what it's like for me.

Stephen, 11

I feel horrible and sick of being handicapped — in other words bored silly.

Mark Fitzgerald, 16

Sometimes you feel like telling the world to get lost. Being handicapped is like being chained to something.

Martyn Morecroft, 16

I would like people to know that "What you've never had you don't miss" is not true. I do miss not being able to ride a bike or skateboard. I also miss not being able to do little things like splashing in rain puddles or being able to ride on a double decker bus. I would like them to understand what it is like to have to spend a large part of your childhood in hospital, but I would not wish it upon them. *Heather Jones*

I think it's dumb to be a slow learner.
I don't like to be me.
It feels awful to be handicapped.
Some of us have problems.
Lots of us have no friends.
Some kids called us rejects.
I feel dumb to be behind.
Some kids throw books and erasers at me. *Bob Jansen*

Heather

What I feel when I am walking by myself along the streets of Buenos Aires is that I am walking towards the end of my deafness which is not so far away. Sometimes, I also feel that I am born again and that I can hear.
Although I am surrounded by people who can hear I feel I am alone in the world. Maybe I feel my soul is crying over my deafness.
I feel that in my lifetime I will not recover my hearing and I try not to feel this because it tortures me. *Carlos Rodriguez, 16*

My worst experience of being in a wheelchair happened when I was eight years old. I was in hospital and two nurses were tidying my bed when one said to the other "Isn't it a shame that she'll never be able to walk?" The other said, "Yes it is." Then they went. Up to that moment I had always believed that one day I would be able to walk. I had no idea that I was going to have to spend the rest of my life in a wheelchair. People seem to think that if you have always been in a wheelchair that you don't have to learn to accept it, but they are wrong because I then had to learn to accept it. *Heather Jones*

22

This is me the way people see me – One part of me almost missing – Useless. I hate it!

Mutinda Kimilu, 9

The Joy I Lost For Ever

I really wish I were healthy and had my left hand. Nobody knows how much I'd like my life to be better, like those who are strong and healthy.
Everybody enjoys living happily, but not me. My life is different. People sometimes do me harm by laughing at me. It is very painful for me and I'd like to avoid moments like this at any cost. When it is warm I'd like to put on a blouse with short sleeves, but I can't. I am simply ashamed.
I hate anybody staring at me and seeing the lack of my left arm. I am very sorry then, the older I am the more painful it is to me.   *Elzbieta Sobiech*

Cripples are at the very end in life's queue. A cripple becomes frightened because he is always visible. He can't hide himself in the crowd of normal people. He feels like a human standing in the middle of a road in the traffic. Life is hard and difficult and only the strongest of us can go through it and they can only count on themselves.   *Tadeusz Wieszczura, 17*

Watching others play

During breaks I could never run with the other children. I stayed alone in the classroom. I was feeling very lonely and very sad. Also, during the physical training I sat alone and very sad because I could not exercise with the others.

Kazimierz Susicki, 12

Sometimes when I see my brother playing I feel sad because I cannot do the same. I don't like to go outside because all I can do is sit there and watch him. *Julie Healey*

Whenever I watch healthy children and see how they run, play hopscotch and ride bicycles it seems to me between them and me there is a thick wall which is difficult to break down. *Grazyna Lipska, 16*

The thing I don't like about being handicapped is that the other boys are always running and I can never catch up with them. *Michael Hayes, 9*

Sometimes when I see my friends go to the swimming baths I wish I could swim but instead I go and watch them. But it is not the same as it would be if I could join in. *Carol Screeton*
Carol has a heart condition.

When I first went home at weekends I was very resentful of all the things that my sister could do. I would love to do some of those things. I get very frustrated if things do not go right all of the time, and that is nearly every day. *Wendy Allen, 14*

◄Renata Rusitowicz

Feeling like a stranger

I feel different.
I don't feel like a person.
The children from across the road kept calling me names
And I never want to go out with my mum and dad.
I just sit by myself.
I see people walking by, I don't feel as if I'm wanted.
I feel like half a person.
I don't feel that my legs are there.
I feel that my legs are like lead.
And like they shouldn't be there at all.
I just sit and think how wonderful to be walking.
And I feel that my legs are invisible.
I just like being on my own in a room by myself. And being very silent.
I stay in bed on Saturday and think.
If I shout I don't mean to shout.
I love my family really.
And they love me.
Sometimes I like to stay in the house when mum goes to the shop.
I like being by my own, it's sometimes very quiet in the house.

Annette Mottershaw, 17

A crippled person is usually alone. Although he has friends and he enjoys playing and talking it is not the same life as that of a healthy man. Those who become cripples feel like strangers from a lower class. For them healthy people seem far away, living on a different and beautiful world. People sometimes try to understand us but they are usually unsuccessful. They either pretend understanding or express pity.   *Tadeusz Wieszczura, 17*

I'm proud to be me. I like to be honest and be truthful. I wish people could accept me for who I am.
If I liked school and liked all the teachers it would be a whole lot easier than now. I just can't get along with other people. I can't talk to them as easy as I can some others. I like my friends to talk to me and to love me. I love them and care for them. But people don't seems to care for me. I would like to have more patience with myself and more other people. I am proud of being me.

Shirley

Tam Kwok Choi

Us and them

Today my teacher told us that this year will be the International Year of Infirm People. She actually said, "not fully dextrous", but I knew what was written: "Infirm". And I get excited again. Infirm, disabled, and compassionate expressions on people's faces. Images like these have persecuted me since my childhood. They give names to us. They organise holidays for us. They teach us. Always they, they, they . . .

Yet it's possible that it could be completely otherwise. Then we wouldn't be divided into two separated groups. I think we are all the same. I want to believe that. I must believe that.

Why do I always think about hearing people as "they"? Why don't I think "we"?

One person taught me that everybody has faults. I have a lot of faults. The most important one is that I don't hear. But should that detach me from people around me? I don't think so. Why, therefore, does it?

They maintain that we are incomprehensible. Yes, it's true.

They say that it's necessary to lend us a hand. And they are right again.

But they live to help us, they have organised this world for us in this way. It's good that we can learn, but why so

far from our homes? My home has always meant for me big expeditions and moments of happiness. But I have always lived in boarding establishments. Even here it isn't so bad, it's only a pity that everything is so surrounded by regulations. That irritates, all the more you want to go home. Go home, where you can sleep for a long time and do nothing. And then at last the time comes to go home:

First day — how pleasant
Second day — it's magnificent
Third day — it starts to get dull
Fourth day — I begin to long to be back
Fifth day — I want to see my friends!

Then I'm with my schoolmates again. We begin to relate. We talk without ceasing. It's magnificent. And it will be so till the time when I begin to pine for my mother, father, brothers and sisters again. When I start to think about that somewhere which is my home. Home, where there aren't regulations for every minute. Home, where I can even do nothing. It's a pity that it's impossible to connect my home and my world.

Then perhaps I'd stop thinking about hearing people as "they". Then perhaps I wouldn't get excited about the world. Nor about myself and that I'm different. Nor about them, and the many things that divide us.

◀ Iwona Koltuniak

Hanna Pastucha, 18

29

Feeling left out

I would like people to talk to me when I meet them. When people don't know me they won't look at me or talk to me. I wish they would talk to me because I want to talk to them. Sometimes I start to talk to people but they don't listen or talk back to me. I try and stand or sit tall so they will hear me. I want people to talk to me more often because I like people.

John Wilson, 9

John is from New Zealand and has cerebral palsy. He dictated these words to his mom because writing takes so long. He has just had an operation "which has given him the blessing of being able to walk after-a-fashion, with the help of a walking frame."

We are willing to participate, longing to give like everyone else, but are we given the chance to? We are so often despised and regarded as fools.
We are not all long-suffering introverts. We're entitled to live. Let us live!
Lick *our* shoes for once. This is a plea for acceptance. If you deny us that right, we may as well be classed as the living dead.   *Velma Sylvan, 16*

I watch the so-called normal sighted people and I admire them and at the same time I envy them their sure pace and other natural skills impossible for me to perform. In my dreams I often see myself as a sailor or a sports champion, but very soon I realize these are only dreams. Coming back to the real world, I know I must learn and get good results in order to go to a good secondary school.
Sometimes I feel that people with good sight can see a different world than I do here. When I find myself among such people I feel I am not needed and nobody cares about me.   *Sylwester Cis, 14*

I feel scared to death.
It's not that the people aren't nice, 'cause they really are.
It's the funny feeling of being something you're not,
Laughing when you really think it is not funny,
And being everybody's DUMMY just to fit in.
It's being left in the cold by all whom you thought you loved.
It is like everyone you thought you loved giving up on you.
So you walk around and what is on your face is a stranger to your heart.

Halina Dudzic

◄*Antonia Chalupechy*

31

Outsider

You take a walk on the streets of Warsaw and Cracow, Paris and New York. You live in the world of silence. You are surrounded by hearing people who you don't understand. You are always alone near them. They have *their* affairs, *their* troubles, *their* interests. They go to the theatre, they hear music at concerts, they go to pictures. And you? You always feel bored at home. You sit and sit. What else can you do? You leave the house. In the street people are talking, but what is the subject of their conversation? You don't know because you see only their quickly-moving lips. Why are they laughing? Why do they argue and why are they sad? YOU HEAR NOTHING, YOU UNDERSTAND NOTHING. For you words are only movements of the lips. They watch interesting films on television and you don't understand. They hear information on the radio. And you? You aren't

very fond of reading because you don't understand all the words. There is not always somebody who can help you and translate. When you go to the cinema, you must choose films with lively action and with sub-titles because otherwise you won't understand.
Sometimes you're angry because their life is easier than yours. Sometimes you reflect why just you were born deaf. People with hearing can work in all the professions they want. They can be sailors, drivers and actors.
Sometimes you would like to talk with hearing people. When you were small you often talked with hearing friends. But you know that they not always *can* and not always *want* to understand you. Therefore you flee to your world. To people who talk with the aid of hands and have similar troubles and pleasures. Among them you feel good.
But I think that it ought to be a little different. Deaf people should endeavour to get out of the world of silence. From childhood they must learn to write correctly, to lip read and to talk. They must read a lot of books, retain new and difficult words, make an effort to learn more and more. And then maybe *our* world won't be so greatly separated from *their* world. And then they will stop being like inhabitants of another planet.
FOR WE ALL LIVE ON ONE EARTH.

Marek Gajdulewicz, 15

Theeradet Srisopa, 12 ▶

I'm happy to be me

Some think I'm different. I'm not. I will never feel the sand between my toes but I am thankful I'm alive no matter how I am or how bad my handicap is. I'm glad I'm living.

Colleen Henley, 17

As for me, I feel completely normal. Like every boy of my age, I have my interests and my hobbies. I love nature, in particular, animals. I have a lot of friends who share my delight in nature. I love reading as well, and I like studying, not only what is essential at school, but also adventure books and geographical ones dealing with voyages and travel to foreign lands. The book — that is my friend.

Three cheers for 1981, dedicated to us the handicapped.

Zdenek Kasparik, 15

I sort of like being handicapped because I went to camp and stayed over for ten nights, and it's a handicapped camp and no regular kids go there. You go swimming in a heated pool and it's sort of like a homemade hotel, so I'm sort of lucky that I could go there because I'm handicapped, but there's no regular people there. Even though I can't play with my friends and all that, when they're riding around and everything and I want to talk to them about something, I think of other things to do such as play with my sister, play games by myself, read books, listen to my tape recorder, watch T.V., play barbie's and, well, these are some of the suggestions I can do. It's just that sometimes I get fed up.

Jordy Davis, 9

"Sharon, What are your three wishes?"
"Me? One. To meet all the pop stars I like. Two. To see Elvis Presley's grave. Three. To have an alsation".
"You wouldn't choose to walk perfectly?"
"No I'm used to the way I am now."
"So you mean you'd rather see Elvis Presley's grave?"
"Yes — well if everybody were normal it would be pretty boring wouldn't it? We're original we are."

Sharon

Vanina E Caporicci, 12

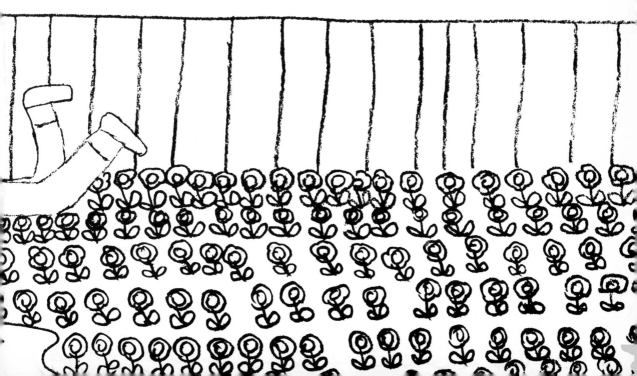

I'm happy to be me

I Feel Special
I am lucky to be me,
For I have friends and I can talk
To others, with an understanding that
Is not given to all. I feel secure
In my surroundings, my community,
My church, and knowing what I cannot do.
I feel special.

Raoul Hickey

I was a sad case of a road accident about seven years ago. Since I was paralysed I have been to some places where people who can walk have never been. I have been to Holland three times. People say that you can't play football. When I say yes I can you could knock them down with a feather. I play basketball, fencing and any other games.
I had some great times when I was able to walk but since I have been in a wheelchair I have had the happiest years of my life. The worst has yet to come, so my mother says. But I do not mind if it carries on like this at all.
Paul Gregory, 15

I like fishing and I love watching ice hockey, my favourite team is the Montreal Canadians (they are the best you know). I like to drive our boat with some help from my Dad. I sleep in the same room with my brother Mark. I have four brothers who are very athletic. We play lots of games. I can beat them in football . . . that is "electronic" football, ha, ha. My two sisters are real pests sometimes but I guess that is to be expected from all sisters. I am the only handicapped in my family but I don't feel any different. The only difference is that I am smarter than they are, ha, ha. I enjoy watching television. My favourite show is "Buck Rodgers".
Joseph Dawson, 12

To be happy is to be healthy, is to have a house instead of a shed, is to like peace and hate wars. To be happy is to be able to come to school to learn to read and write and to see friends. And to have a car, to go to the beach and make picnics in the woods. To be happy is to have the love of the parents, of the brothers, of the schoolteachers, of the mates and of everybody.
Cristina M, 12

Why do people take us for unhappy children for we are as happy as any others.
Bertrand Stephane, 12

◀ *Suzie Burston, 9*

Triumph!

When I was born they thought I was gonna die. But I fooled them, even my parents.

Lori Brezina

My most fantastic success was to find a method of getting myself into a bath!

Alain Banas, 16

My biggest triumph and the best day in my life was when I walked on my own with crutches. When I was a little girl I was unlucky as I was ill with arthritis. I have been in hospital many times to have treatment.
I can help my mother sometimes and can look after my baby sister. I will never forget June 13th 1980 it was my happiest day in my life.

Nicola Holden, 7

My main aim in life is to become an artist. I paint in oil paints with a brush in my mouth. People often say "I don't know how she does it. I can't even do that with my own two hands." I mostly take that as a compliment.

Cathy Katon

My greatest achievement was six years ago when I did my first play which was 'Snow White and the Seven Dwarfs' in which I played the dame. Some able-bodied people think that we can't do it, but they're wrong, we can. I have done four plays since then. It feels like another world with the make-up and the lights. You tend to think that you are in another century such as when I was Sherlock Holmes in 'The Hound of the Baskervilles'. We don't write the plays ourselves, the drama teacher writes them for us. We do our plays every two years and they are great fun.
They are great fun because we tend to forget that we are in wheelchairs with problems with our arms and legs and we pretend we are someone else. These are the things that an able-bodied person does not understand. That I think is a great pity because we would like them to know that we can do these things ourselves. So please think again because when you see us perform you will say to yourself, 'Well I was wrong; they *can* perform plays themselves'.

Ian McArdle, 14

Petr Suska

I use a board with the alphabet on it to speak. I cannot feed myself or have a bath by myself but I can build blocks and type with my toes. People take things for granted where I find it hard just to feed myself.

My proudest moment was when I finally achieved the art of folding a serviette with the help of my headpiece and a frame which held it in place for me. It took me three months to achieve this but now I can do it like all the other young people.

Glen Hill

Triumph!

When I was born I had lack of oxygen. When the doctor gave me more he overdid it. It went to my brain and affected the use of my hands and legs. A doctor once told my late mother that I would never be able to get up and walk. When I heard this at the age of six or seven, that was it. I set my mind to that one day I would prove them all wrong. Then two years later I did just that. With the help of my best friend, Beryl, and my physiotherapist, I actually got up and walked. I'll admit that it wasn't the best way of walking, but the important thing to me is that I had gotten to my destination. After several years of practice I am able to walk around pushing a chair. That's the most important thing to me.

Cathy Katon

A moment of victory? So far, the best moment of victory for me was when I found out, one week after I'd taken the entrance examination on a secondary school, I'd become a student of this school. I couldn't even believe it! The long preparation, the hard hours of studying, the grind, it all was worth it. I kept on repeating: "I will be studying. My dream came true!"

Iva Merhautová

Nicola and I got up out of bed on Monday. I thought that we would give mum a surprise so Nicola dressed me for her with me standing beside my wheelchair holding on the back of it she dressed the most of me on the bed. And boy was mum pleased.
This was the first time I ever got dressed at home without my mother helping me.

Debby Knight

My greatest achievement was learning to dress and undress myself. Until I was eleven years old, people at home or in school had to help me to dress from head to foot and put my shoes on for me. After many months of hard work, I was able to dress myself completely. I was very pleased that I had achieved something which was worthwhile.

Tracey Lucas, 16

When I was small, I had a disease called spinal meningitis. It affected my brain and I was paralyzed on the right. The doctor told my parents not to train me or put shoes on me. I would be nothing but a vegetable. But I fooled them all. I could go to school and be trained.

Patrick M Jennings

Ji Hae Yang, 11 ▶

I'd like to help

Hi there! My name is Erica and I am disabled. I am writing this contribution in the hope of telling people all over the world something about disabled people and how we like to be treated.

Many of us want to be independent and treated like normal human beings, with the odd bit of help once in a while. Many people do lots of things to help us, with raising money to get equipment we sometimes need. But I think it is a much greater thing when we raise money for you.

Yesterday, Tuesday, 4th November, we did a sponsored walk around our school to help look after some of our endangered animals. All the teachers and helpers joined in, either pushing wheelchairs or cheering us on.

Erica Lockhart, 13

My dream is to be a nurse. If I were a nurse I could cure all the children. I would be very kind to all the children with hearing defects like me. I really want to be a nurse so that I can help everyone.   *Sang-Hee Kim, 9*

I would like to be a nurse because I would like to help sick people in any way I could. I wouldn't mind washing and drying the clothes or dishes. I would cook too and give needles and medicine.   *Corinna Ehrmann*

When I was young I went to hospital on my mother's back and that's all I did.
Auditory paralysis*, I didn't know what it was because I was very small. Mother spent those days in tears. So I became familiar with tears. But because my mother did so much for me, I became a diligent student. Mother tried not to feel desperate, but instead she gave me emotional support. Even today, with a bright feeling in my heart, I study more diligently than normal children.
I have one desire. That is to become a teacher at my school. The students I will teach will like me to teach them hopefulness. I want to be the fertilizer of their hope.
I want to pray, "Please God, give me the wisdom and strength to fulfil my desire."   *Jeong Nan Park*
**causes loss of hearing*

I want to prove that even though I do not hear, I work and enjoy my life as all hearing people do. My life will be tough and I have to get prepared now. I want to convince people that a deaf person can sometimes work better and be a better human being than some normal ones.   *Ivana Jahodova*

A handicapped can also help people as you see in the picture. These children are going to school helping each other in Joytown School in Kenya.

Peter Ngángá Githua

My moment of greatest pride is when I am entrusted with household or other jobs and I can do them without any damage. In spite of being handicapped, the service I want to give when I am grown up is to help others, handicapped or not.

Levet Martine, 15

At home I try to be useful. I make cups of tea and dust, but sometimes I get in the way.

Kevin Dowling

Now I'd like to tell you my joys. To some they may seem small but to me they are big. My first joy is being able to stand for a few seconds or take my first step or even being able to do the housework in some way.

My most important joy is seeing my family happy. That's my only joy that really means a lot to me; seeing the smiles on my family's faces.

Colleen Henley, 17

43

I will fight

I've had to seek out
Further safe passages,
Turn away when mindless children
Stare and whisper.
Mentally it hurts
Though they do not understand,
They think life's one easy road,
No bumps, no potholes, no troubles at all.
These pressures are like mountains,
Never ending;
But you have to keep on going
Staring life right in the face,
Overcoming every obstacle
Risking everything.

Richard Field, 15

Hurt is how I feel.
But what is done is done is done.
The biggest problem is knowing
I can handle it
But knowing you don't have the patience.
Thinking I can handle it, but feeling you can't handle it.
It hurts to know that you don't have the patience.
But I do.
Halina Dudzic, 18

Hope! Whenever I hear that word, my heart starts pounding in my breast
and feels like it will swell up like a balloon.
But I am abnormal, so I cannot join normal people. Most deaf people are
frustrated in the face of hope and are leading desperate lives with bitter
hearts. I want to shout, "Deaf people too should live in hope!" This may be
talking to myself. I don't know. People who have lost hope are like people
who have lost their souls. I will live with hope even though I can feel my
hope perishing like water bubbles.
Eun Seong Son, 14

Jonathan Kaye, 9

Smiling is the answer
When I really want to cry
Chrissie Chadwick

45

*This is Mommie's plant. I like it 'cause
we both are growing.*

Theresa Houston, 5

46

I'm okay

To be me it is like not being able to see. It is like being blindfolded. It is like something is blocking your eyes out of the way. It is like somebody saying get out of my way. I'm trying to see, but I do Okay. If I cannot see the pictures or what's going on I ask. If I cannot see something I can touch it. If I cannot see where things are I feel. If I cannot find something someone tells me.

Laney Troutman, 8

My name is Autumn. I have to wear different shoes than everybody else. Every now and then I like my braces. Kids sometimes stare at me. It feels bad. I wish I could wear sneakers. I feel like telling them what it is like to wear my shoes.
Kids used to stare at my face but they don't now because the doctor fixed it. He has more operations to do and then I will look prettier.
I like being Autumn because I have a smarter brain than other kids.
This is a rainbow. It has a doorknob because a rainbow is happiness and I can get in.

Autumn Rosenberg, 6

Autumn

Brave people

"What's been the nicest thing that's happened to you?"
"Meeting other people like me. Like when I was in hospital last year there were loads of people with brittle bones worse than me. We all used to sit round saying "Well I've broken my leg so many times. We were all in competition with each other. There was this boy in there and he had broken his legs 107 times. I was about the second highest. Only 98

Sharon Kennedy, 16

It was unlucky of me to be born different and when I grow up, it will be hard to receive the strange pitiful looks. But I am well prepared to accept this rugged and rocky road of life.

Kwok Sui Yee, 17

Kerry, 9

I was a very sick baby and my Mum and Dad never thought I would make it through all this, but I will. I will, don't worry, I will. I'll try the best I can, that's the main thing.

I think I'm a very special person, even though I get in trouble a lot. That doesn't mean anything, that doesn't mean I'm dumb or anything.

I'm smart and I just know that I have a handicap. I don't say to myself, "Oh, poor Jordy, poor Jordy, she can't do it so she's got to be helped". First I try, and if I can't do it, then I really call, but if I can do it then I don't call. Maybe I'll cheat a couple of times, but that's natural.

And I hope you have a good day, cause I'm not finished talking.

Everybody is handicapped but in certain ways. Some handicaps show, some handicaps are in a person's mind. Only mine shows and I still have to work around it. I'll walk, but I won't walk perfectly. Sometimes I wonder why God gave me a handicap. I think if He gave me a handicap then there is a real good reason why. I don't know if He did, but I just have to work around it, even though I sometimes say "Jordy give up, you can't do it". Down deep I know I can, so winning and losing aren't the best things. Have you tried your hardest is the question.

Jordy Davis, 9

The beginning was very hard, but I made it. My parents and my teacher helped me very much: they encouraged me, added some self-confidence, supported me. I won't forget it as long as I live. Now all of us — them and me — believe I'll successfully finish secondary school and my moment of victory will come in two years when I'll graduate. That's why I'm so happy. But there are also days when I'm sad and I don't feel well. Those are days when I realize how much I'm being cheated of life when I do not hear. I can't listen to the music, I can't hear the birds singing, I can't watch TV or go to the theatre or a concert. But I don't want to give in. I want to — and I will — fight. I want to live a beautiful life and I'll do everything to realize it.

Iva Merhautová

The importance of a disabled person keeping a sense of humour cannot be stressed too strongly. If there is one thing I cannot stand, it is someone who is disabled feeling sorry for themselves just because they are disabled. Come to that, I do not like anybody feeling sorry for themselves for no reason, and just because of disability is *no reason whatsoever*. It is absolutely vital that a disabled person thinks positively all the time, and keeps looking on the bright side. In fact, what I always say is, look beyond the end of your nose and you will find someone who is a hell of a lot worse off than you, and it is meeting these people and talking to them, and helping them come to terms with their problems, that makes me happiest.

Brian Wilson, 17

Great sports

The only thing I cannot do is walk. I can do things anyone can do plus more. I have been in a wheelchair for one year now and have learned to adapt, I now use my wheelchair as a pair of legs. I play many sports including football (I play in the goals), cricket, basketball and archery. I can also swim. I enjoy swimming and am quite a good swimmer. I run a disco on a Wednesday dinner time and Thursday night at our youth club. Our youth club is a two hour session where some children from our school come and enjoy themselves. There is snooker, table tennis, TV and the disco.

Gwyn Davies, 13

My proudest moment was when I went to Stoke Mandeville swimming gala and broke two British records. The gala is held every year at Stoke Mandeville stadium. My race was Event 9 and when my breaststroke race finally came the boy next to me went in front first. Halfway down the pool I went in front by a few inches, then I went further and further in front and I touched the end to win the race. The announcer read out the results and then he said that I had broken the British record.

My second race was the backstroke. The starter fired his gun and the race began. This time I went in front first. The boy next to me was slowly creeping upon on me so I pushed with all my strength and went further in front. Suddenly I touched the end to win the race. I was getting out of the pool when the announcer read out that I had broken another British record, so I went back to my bench feeling very proud.
Stephen Rimmer

Me playing rugby or soccer
Gavin Foulsham

I would like to enter all kinds of sports. First and foremost I would like to do track events. Running is a sport which is not very exciting but something that keeps you fit and also brings the best competition out of people.

To be able to run in track events and also compete in field events is something which can encourage individuals to achieve their ambitions in life. If I weren't in a wheelchair I would like to play for my favourite football team which is Ipswich Town.

The thing that I can achieve is snooker where I am the second best in Britain in a wheelchair. I like doing discus because it gets your arms strong and I like doing all the rest of the sports like wheelchair slalom where you have to go as fast as you can in and out of obstacles going backwards and forwards. Javelin is another of my favourite sports. It is like discus but you throw it in front of you as far as you can. With discus you throw it from your side as far as you can until it drops near in front of you. It's really great to be picked for the Stoke Mandeville Games for the Disabled where we do the same things like Sebastian Coe who is a runner. Although I would really like to be a proper athlete I do enjoy the sports designed for disabled people just the same.

Mark Carter, 16

Mark and Stephen

Young Sug Hong, 10 ▶

생일

고 3 의 3 반

김 영민

그 날은 1월 17일 바로 내 생일이었읍니다. 때마침 하늘에서는 솜같은 꽃송이가 펑펑 쏟아지고 있었읍니다. 하늘 나라에 있는 천사들이 내 생일을 축복해 주는 것이구나 생각하며 하염없이 창밖을 내다보고 있는데 영민아 밥먹어 하시며 어머니께서 내 등을 두들겨 주고 계셨읍니다.

식당에 내려가니 아빠 동생들이 식탁앞에 앉았다가 손뼉을 쳐 주었읍니다. 내 얼굴은 홍당무처럼 빨갛게 되었어요. 식탁 위에는 보통때 보다 조금도 다름이 없는 음식들이 놓여 있었읍니다. 내가 좋아하는 닭요지도 케이키도 없었읍니다 그러나 나는 조금도 섭섭하지가 않았어요. 일부러 어머니게 부탁을 드려서 화려하지 않은 식탁을 차려 달라

The need to give back

It was the seventeenth of January, my birthday. On that day, the snow was falling from the sky like balls of cotton.

I was looking out of the window, thinking how the angels in the sky country were celebrating my birthday. Suddenly my mother was tapping me on the back saying "Young Min! Come eat!"

My father, brothers, and sisters were waiting at the table. They clapped their hands when I entered the dining room. I blushed. Dinner was on the table as usual. My favorite foods, chicken and cake, were not there. But I was not sorry, because I had asked my mother not to make special food for me.

When I recall my birthday last year, mother made many special foods and invited my friends. We ate many delicious foods and played happily until the nighttime. And finally I went out to the bus stop to see my friends off. It was very cold that day. I was humming happily to myself on the way home, when I saw a very sad scene. A woman with no legs, holding a baby in her arms, was begging under the branches of an old dead tree. I had no money, so I couldn't help her. Weeping, I went home. All that night I sat at my desk and I made up my mind that though I am deaf, I will work hard to help those who are more unhappy than I.

Not to forget that, from now on, instead of celebration, my birthday will be a day to serve and help others more unfortunate than I.

Young Min Kim, 17, Republic of Korea

◀*Young Min Kim's letter*

Understanding through suffering

. . . the most important advantage of losing one's sight — you learn that people's appearances don't matter, and that it's far more important what they are as a person.

Anne Carter, 11

When I was just a little girl, my mother often used to be sad. Once I asked her: "Mom, why are you so sad?" My mother answered because Vojta and you don't hear. I told her: "It doesn't matter mom, don't be sad. Votja and I will be good at school and you will be happy. In school I have many friends, they understand me and we have a lot of fun together.'   *Ivana Jahodová*

I was born with cerebral palsy so really do not know what it's like to run and play like normal kids. But I'm glad that I am alive so I can show other people how lucky they are to be able to walk. And I truly believe that God made me this way because he knows I could live with the disability.

James Hanoski, 17

The most important thing
In the whole world
May be our wisdom
Because it helps make things of convenience.

Each of us has his very own thing
Most valuable in the world
To take good care of
And to use very well.   *Yu Chul Won*

How should I live? How should man live? What is life? Before I suffered from heart trouble I had never thought of such things, so happy a life, it seems to me, I had been living. But today I often find myself thinking about how to live.
In my view man should spend each day doing his best to his heart's content. Otherwise man would be, as it were, a breathing doll. I myself am not satisfied with my life, so I am also a kind of breathing doll. If I were in good health, I could run about in the playground, or I could go on a trip with my family. If I were strong enough I would go on to a high school. As it is, I am in hospital.
Recently, however, I have come to bear a belief like this. Although I am not healthy physically, I am healthy mentally. So I should like to lead a happy, full life reading books or enjoying a variety of things. And I think I will write essays or compose poems for songs. By doing so, I will be able to make my life more fruitful.   *Kaoru Kubota*

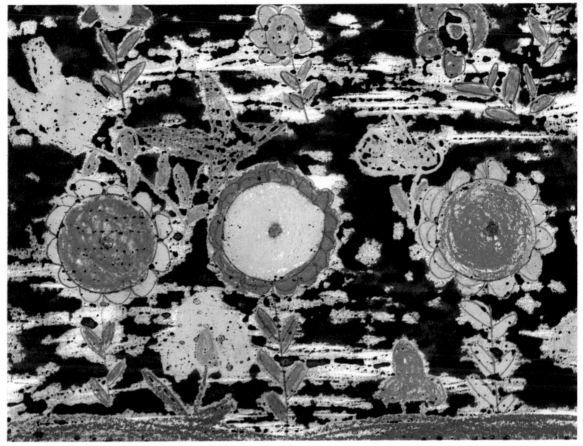

My hands are part of my body and they are guided by my heart . . .
My hands are my best friends; I like them very much, because I have a
disability in my lower limbs. If I didn't have hands,I couldn't walk with
crutches so I wouldn't walk at all.
There are hands that start wars and others that make peace. But my hands
will never start wars but they will make peace, they will love the people, the
poor, and sick and that's how all the hands of the world should be.

*'The flowers bloom for us
too' by Alda Covas*

Cecilia, 14

Hello! I am a disabled boy. I wish to be understood and may I tell you my
feelings. We may be disabled but we have our abilities too. I always believe
the value of life is not measured by the length of life but by what one can
achieve during life.
A good friend of mine once said "Life is like a 'comet'. It will light up and
brighten the whole world, even though it may sparkle and disappear in a
second."
I wish people would give us the opportunity to reach our potential. I, too,
sincerely hope all the disabled could understand the meaning of those words
and try their best to contribute to their society. *Wong Chi Hang, 15*

Chris with his teacher.

ABOVE: Chris uses a mouthstick to type all his schoolwork.

LEFT: Chris with his sister, Tammy.

The big crash

At the age of three I was learning to ride a two-wheeled bike. I fell a lot of times, but finally I didn't fall anymore. So I rode all around.

When I was five we moved to the country. I really liked the country because I could play in the sand and fly kites in the summer. In the wintertime I used to really have fun skating outside on ice in front of our house. On weekends I used to go to ski down the neighbor's hill. Some afternoons after school I used to go tobogganning down the neighbor's hill. Just after my eighth birthday my uncle suggested that we go tobogganning. After we were tobogganning for an hour I wanted to go home but my sister didn't want to go home. So I went down once more. At the bottom of the hill I hit a telephone pole head first and broke my neck and blacked out. I woke up when they were taking me out of the ambulance. Then they put me to sleep. I woke up in a hospital bed in Edmonton, Alberta, Canada. I tried to move my arms, but I couldn't.

So I just lay there. Soon the doctor came and told me I was paralysed, which meant I can't move from my shoulders down. I was in the hospital three months, thinking about my parents and my dog. After those three months, I went to the Glenrose School Hospital. When I got there a girl named Elsie gave me a tour of the place. A guy named Carl turned out to be my best friend. I began school here the following September.

I came to Glenrose School Hospital because I needed physiotherapy and occupational therapy. Physiotherapy keeps my muscles loose so they don't tighten up. Prosthetics fit a body brace around me so I can sit up straight.

Occupational therapists made me a mouthstick about thirty centimeters long with a plastic piece that goes in my mouth and a rubber tip to hit the typewriter keys. I operate my electric wheelchair with my head. When I press back with my head my chair goes forward, when I click the red lever and press back the chair goes backward, when I click it again my chair goes forward. When I want to go to the right I press a white pad, when I want to go left, I press the white pad on the left.

When I wake up in the morning my mom does my catheterization, then does my exercises and gets me dressed. Then she sits me up in my wheelchair and I drive into the kitchen where I take my pills. Then I eat breakfast using my feeder plate made by my occupational therapist, then watch T.V. till the school bus comes. At school I do different subjects all day. I can't use a pencil so I type all my work with a mouth stick. At recess I am fed a drink of water. At noon the nurses feed me then catheterize me. After that my friends and I drive around in our wheelchairs. After school the bus drives me home, then I get cathed and we have supper. After supper some days I have suppositories and other days I watch T.V. Sometimes my friends come over and I play cars or games or dinasours with them. If it's not winter we make sand towns. I tell Develin how to make them and he does it for me. After watching T.V. I go to bed.

I will soon be discharged from the Glenrose School Hospital and will be going to a brand new school in my home town, Leduc. I can hardly wait to be back with all my friends.

Christopher Knelsen, 9, Canada

I'm happy!

What I like about being disabled is that I never do eney house work.

Michael Hayes, 9

There's one thing I like about calipers, I can play Space Invaders in the arcades.

Terry Evans, 14

Wearing a hearing aid playing at football does not bother you. When it rains it stops water getting in your ear.

Stuart Laing, 10

It's not nice being handicapped, but I'm not unhappy with my situation as I could have been born a chicken or a duck.

Martin Styles, 10

Mark Carter

Happy endings

Renata

Today I am describing my experiences with a great joy in my heart and tears in my eyes. The ward head, after checking me, assured me that wearing the apparatus would be a matter of only weeks. Despite the fact that the apparatus will now be removed, I will never forget that I have been a girl whom some people called a "cripple".

The complications began when I was seven. One day a doctor visited our school and found I had a spinal curvature. Since then people began watching my back and the children began calling me "the hump-back", although it was not very visible. One day I was walking home with a school girl friend and we began to quarrel. I do not remember what the matter was. But my heart stuck when she said to me, "Go away you hump-back, if not I am going to strike you so that the hump will be straightened". I returned home in tears. My parents asked me what had happened, but I said nothing, only I cried, and in my soul I thought: "My dearest God, when will this suffering end?"

Calling me names like this took place for four years. At last a notification from the sanatorium arrived. My parents were shocked at having to part with me. I didn't think I'd be able to survive the separation.

The worst time was in the Easter holidays. I cried terribly because I wanted to be at table with my parents and this was impossible. But such a moment eventually arrived, and I was to pack my things because

my parents were coming to take me. It was the most happy day in my life. On my return home people looked at me terribly, but my girlfriends of the same age were glad I was back. This lasted very shortly like a good film, then the nickname "hump-back" appeared again, as well as ridicule. Even a girl who is deaf and dumb used to say to other people by means of sign language that I had a big hump, although she herself was wronged by fate more than I.

Several years passed and a boy one year older than me arrived where I was living. We became friends. Everybody laughed at him because he was not ashamed to talk to a cripple. Was not she hump-backed? But although the boy was younger than they were, he was much wiser. One day the doctor told me there was a worsening of the spine, that it was more distorted. A further, longer stay in the sanatorium would be necessary. Besides rehabilitation exercises I would have to wear an apparatus and spend Christmas and New Year at the sanatorium.

It was a great shock to me when I received a notification of going to the sanatorium. I despaired very much. Under the influence of this shock I unfolded the notification a dozen times. The last night before my departure I cried with mother at home, very much. That night I put myself beside the dearest creature of my life, Mother. When she fell asleep I still was crying, wetting the pillow with my tears.

Then the moment of parting with

my home and mother came. After saying me goodbye my mother went to work. I was sitting at the table ready for the travel. Then my father entered the room. I said nothing but burst into tears with terrible despair. As my father is very sensitive to crying he began to comfort me, but he was crying himself.

The first day in the sanatorium was like madness. Then weeks passed and at last came holidays far from home. It was a shock for me. The girls sitting with me at the table were crying, but I not, since I did not want the despair to become even stronger. Only during the night did I despair over the home.

At last the day came when I left the sanatorium. I started the life of a cripple among healthy children. They began ridiculing me. Among other things I heard: "a clown", "she walks like a dog in leash". My parents tried to comfort me, but it was not easy. I could not understand it. I became an egoist, I avoided people, even those well-mannered. One day I read in the newspaper about the existence of an institution for crippled children in Police. When I returned home I told my parents about this. We all decided that I should go there. I was admitted, and it is simply splendid, because they do not laugh at my illness because everybody here is more or less wronged by the fate. Looking at all the conflicts which I have experienced, I know what it means to be a cripple whom everybody spurns and laughs at. Now I know some people are contemptible and thoughtless. They do not know what they can expect from life, and that life is like a long film that sometimes can end tragically.

Although I am now almost in good health I shall never forget those experiences among the healthy people.

Renata Klusiewicz, 15, Poland

Another Happy Ending

When I was around two years old my eyes were bad and it was getting worse and worse and one morning when I woke up I screamed so loud that Mom thought I was taking a heart attack, but when I told her that I could not see anything she said to come down and told me that I was blind. That's all I could see was black, I thought I wouldn't see light in my life again. The years past and I went to blind school every single day.

Lori

Then Dad said why don't we take a trip to Disneyland. Well I wasn't feeling too well cause I was catching the flu so I said let's go next week. When the week had come to go at Disneyland we had everything packed. We started to go. When we got there I could feel the excitement all over me. The third day I was there I was on the Merrygoround and my sight came back to me. I was so glad, I started to cry! (I can see, I can see!) I never forget that day when I got my sight back. It was my happiest day in the whole wide world.

Lori Poirier, 11

Family support

When my Mum had me everybody told her to get rid of me because I was handicapped. She's kept me, she runs me up to the hospital and comes to see me and all that. It's her I'd like to thank most of all.   *Sharon Kennedy*

Dear Mum,
I would just like to thank you for being my mum. For being nearby when I need help, and for showing how much you love and care for me. I know that you sometimes become tired but you always carry on. You help me to cope with my handicap by talking to me and making me understand my problems. Whenever I am ill or just under the weather, you nurse me in every way you can because you care. You will always remain in my memory as long as I live. You care for me and for that I will never forget you. Never once have you forgotten my birthday and for that you deserve the biggest bunch of red roses in the world.
With lots of love and kisses,
x x x x x
Christine   *Christine Brighton, 13*

My family copes with all my problems very well. They treat me as an ordinary, able-bodied person as much as they possibly can. I don't have any sympathy from my family and friends unless I really need it. To them, I am no different from anyone else.   *Tracey Lucas, 16*

I didn't realise I was born with spina bifida until my Mom told me. I started to cry but my mother told me not to worry and she has made me smile again.
Daphne Mitchell, 13

My family have been affected in many ways. They are the ones that have had to watch me go in and out of hospital continuously throughout my life and watch me suffer. They are the ones who have tried to help me cope with my disability and particularly my mom has had to struggle to try and make me as independent as possible and I thank her for it. I'm glad she didn't give up the struggle, especially when I look at some of my friends.
Then there's my brother and sister who have had to help in various different ways, but I think the hardest struggle has been for all of us. This was not only because we had to come to terms with my handicap, but also coping with life when my father died, when I was nine months old.
All my life my mom has struggled and struggled. My family have been the ones who have watched me struggle myself to try and cope with my disability and have tried to help me in any way they can.
The public are another problem.   *Andrew Butterworth, 16*

Father

How can I put the way I feel
down on paper?
Sure, he never shows his feelings publicly,
but they are there.
Both of my parents have been through a lot
because of me.
But one thing I learned is how much they care.
Before I was not sure.
But it is funny how, when there is a crisis
everyone sticks together.
I guess I had an experience to learn how much I
have going for me.

Halina Dudzic

Mother

The only person that I know who has a heart of gold
and spreads her love around like it was free.
When she has something to say be sure and listen
because she has your well-being in mind.
Sure, you can say you can live your own life,
But when there is trouble she is the first person
to run to for shelter and help.
She is always ready to help
you to get out of the mess you have gotten yourself in.

Halina Dudzic

Sharon, 10

Mothers

Parents are people whose lives are physically and mentally linked to their
children. Women rear large families and fathers earn the money necessary
to support them.
A mother however plays a very important role, she it is who teaches her
child the first lesson on life. My mother is especially lovely, as it was she
who encouraged me down the years. A fiery person would be no use to me,
only patience could help a spastic. People will never know what she really
did, she consoled me when I was sad, she played with me when I was glad,
she taught me all I know about people and their problems. A person finds
other friends in life, but nobody will ever replace their mother.

Christopher Nolan

Christopher Nolan is spastic. Up to the age of twelve he could only communicate with
his eyes. Then he learned to type and out poured prose and poetry. His writing has been
collected in the best-selling book "Dam-burst of Dreams". One of the first things he
wrote was this tribute to his mother.

A friend in need

Everyone needs friends but we need them more than most people. We need good friends that we can trust and that we know that we can go to for help.

Lee Garrett, 13

An example of someone who does more to help the disabled than almost anyone else I know, is my cousin Kevin. I am not being biased towards my relations when I say this because I would not write anything I did not truly believe in. He is only twelve years old and people may think that he is also slightly immature, but this is not true at all. In fact exactly the opposite. He never takes advantage of my disability or refers to it in any way. He is kind and helpful when assistance is needed but likes to see me do as much for myself as possible. In other words he sees me as a normal person. Nobody's perfect, he makes revolting coffee.

Brian Wilson, 17

When I was walking one day I met somebody. He said "Want help to get to my house?" I said "Please". When we got there he said "That's funny I live next door". I said "Come over", "Sure", he said. And then we were the best of friends.

Michael Doiron, 10

Some people think they're funny by saying things about me. Take one day when one lad come up to me and said things about me, and my friend said, "Do you want a fight". He walked away.

Terry Evans, 14

Somboon Charnpanit ▶

My friends do not think of me as a person with cerebral palsy. That makes me feel good about me.

Andrey Kinast, 9

Jobs - a chance for tomorrow

I do well in my education. But when I finish learning I will not be able to get a job. A person who is not disabled can do work better than the disabled. In my opinion my problems will not finish until the end of my life.

Abraham Mburu, 17

I like to be treated like everyone else especially at a job interview. They tell me they don't have any more vacancies and they don't give me a chance to explain what I can do.   *Larry Cover, 18*

I had to make up my mind what job to choose. I wanted to become a nurse, but in my case it was impossible so all my plans went in vain. It was horrible to realize that. This was the first moment I really started to think of my life, my health and future. I changed because I noticed how different I was from others and I became very nervous, closed in on myself and broken down.

Lidia Krezelok, 17

I have no difficulties in learning and in the fifth class I was given an award for good results in learning. I frequently think now what nice profession I could take up in the future. Perhaps I could be a pilot? Or, perhaps, I could be a captain of a ship? However, I am fully aware that I shall never be a pilot or seaman. I will have to choose a profession which I am able to carry out and not one which I would like. My Daddy says that I should learn to repair radio and television sets, as this is work which can be done in a sitting position.

Kazimierz Susicki, 12

You've got to be better than the next person. When I wanted a Saturday job, most of them turned me down flat. They'd say "You couldn't manage, you'll hurt yourself." One actually said "You'll frighten away the customer." Finally at an interview I said, "I know you're not going to give me this job", and the woman asked why and I said "Nobody does, because of my disability." Then she called the supervisor and I did get it, answering receptionist and telephone enquiries at a big toy shop.   *David Ruebain*

As I grew older, people began to talk to me about my handicap and show me pictures of other handicapped children. This helped me to understand more clearly why I could only do certain jobs and not others. I was upset at first when I was told that I could not be a nurse or a doctor but although it took me a long time to accept it, eventually I accepted the reasons behind all this and I then set my mind on other types of jobs which I am able to do.

Tracey Lucas, 16

◀ *Cezary Skowroński*

Pro institutions

One of my biggest joys, I think, has been to meet people with the same problems as I have, and to whom I am able to speak.

Kim Preuthun

Life proves that a weak person must be a loser. If physically handicapped people are left alone among healthy people they'll always feel weaker and worse than the others. No wonder cripples prefer staying among the same unhappy ones, not to feel outsiders. *Tadeusz Wieszczura, 17*

I'm a slow learner. I feel sad when I get teased.
I got pushed off a old car roof when I was two
years old and it made me a slow learner. At
Horizon school I do ceramics and woodworking and
lots of fun things. Horizon school is a fun school.
I enjoy school. I have friends that are slow
learners too. I feel everyone cares in this school.

Teresa Stair

My disability is polio, and I have had it since I was one year old. Now that I am in a special school everything is different. I can do so many things that I could never do before. I used to be in an ordinary school and I could only do schoolwork. After lunch all my friends used to run out to the fields and play soccer or basketball, and I used to watch them. Yes, some who didn't like sport stayed and talked to me, but I wanted to play too.

Then, when I came to this special school there was so much I could do — basketball, handball, races, canoeing, horse-riding, swimming and hockey. Unfortunately I can't do these very well because my arm muscles are quite weak and I can't throw the ball high enough to get it in the net, and I can't push myself up slopes.   *Christina Candey, 15*

I live in a boarding school for children with bad eyesight. Here I have friends with a similar defect. Therefore, we feel more comfortable because none of us laughs at one another. Everybody understands the rest of the group and we console one another. We feel the air of kindness around us and good conditions of our life here, but nothing can substitute the warmth of true home.

In our school we have very warm-hearted teachers who help us willingly with our numerous difficulties and cheer us up when we are sad. They want to be like parents to us.   *Zbigniew Karbut, 14*

Yu Chui Fung

Pro normal schools

Some people think that handicapped people should be in institutions and not out but I think that if they can handle themselves, then it should be all right. It bothers me that some people put us in institutions and just throw the key away.

Margaret Clark

Schools are a problem for disabled people because most schools have steps. I think that they ought to have facilities for us as well so that we can go to an ordinary school and mix with non-disabled people. Then when we leave school we'd know people who are not disabled.

Bernadette Hagan, 13

I moved into Stonepark Junior Highschool. This was quite an adjustment for me because at Stonepark the students are regular Junior High students with no noticeable problems. When I first got there, I was a little bit scared because of all the kids running.
But soon I adjusted. The students made me feel very welcome. They assisted me in opening heavy doors and in telling me different things about my new school. The school principal was very helpful in preparing other teachers for our arrival. He showed them different films on the disabled, which some of the students also got a chance to see. It didn't take long before I made many new friends who regarded me as a normal person.

Mike Morrison, 15

John Chilton School is a special physically handicapped school, and Walford High School is a normal school. They are next to each other so that some of the older children can have their lessons at the ordinary school, but they come back for their lunch and other lessons to John Chilton School.
My handicap is that I cannot use my hands at all, but I make up for this disability by using my feet as much as I can. Obviously my feet cannot make up for everything, like feeding myself, dressing myself and playing sports, which I love. You may be wondering how I do my work at Walford School. Well, I overcome this problem by using a special typewriter called a "Possum". I work the Possum with my feet by tapping out a code on two pedals. It is moved from class to class by one of the welfare assistants.
When I first went to the ordinary school I wasn't sure how the other children in my class would accept me. Naturally, at first, they were curious, but when they got to know me better they seemed to accept me. They open the doors for me and help me in different ways, but they talk to me as though I wasn't handicapped.

David Bundy, 14

70

You have to eat when they want you to eat. And what they want you to eat. You can't choose. You can't sleep when you want to. And you have to go to bed when they want you to.

At home I'm only handicapped. Here I'm handicapped and in a prison.

Name withheld

It costs about £10,000 a year to keep a child in a handicapped school. A marginal amount of that could be used to adapt an ordinary school. That way, wheelchair, deaf or blind kids could cope quite well. The economies behind it, the logistics, the social aspect, *everything* points to the integration of handicapped children into ordinary schools.

I think the benefits wouldn't only be for the handicapped child but for the ordinary child as well. One of the most important things I've found is that the total lack of ability to communicate is because of the separation. Ordinary children never see handicapped children and don't know how to deal with them or react to them.

Children normally don't see anyone that's different. So when they do it comes as a shock. They're afraid of someone different. It's not the physical thing, it's the mentality behind it. It's the mentality that someone who doesn't look or behave according to pattern isn't accepted.

Integration is the most important way to aid the handicapped. And don't forget that lots of very mildly handicapped children and children with asthma or epilepsy are needlessly kept in special schools.

David Ruebain

Caroline Skeet, 13

From developing countries

A Story from Kenya

When I became a cripple I knew my life in future would not be easy on this cruel world of ours. I imagined wriggling like a snake on my stomach. Sometimes my mother took me outside to stay there and she went to work. The sun burnt me until they came back.

One day when I was just sitting down I saw a white man coming towards our house. In those days I used to call Europeans policemen. I moved on my stomach to hide in a nearby bush, but the white man had already seen me. When I was hiding I heard him asking my mother to call her family. My mother could not understand because she was illiterate, so she called my older brother who could understand English. They started looking for me. When they found me they took me to the white man. I noticed that he was not a policeman but a Christian missionary.

He told us that he had already heard about me and how I was. He advised my mother not to be worried because he knew that I was going to walk because he had a friend working at Kenyatta hospital.

One week later I was told that I must go to Kenyatta National Hospital where I would meet the doctor. When I arrived I met the doctor and the missionary. I stayed in the hospital until I walked properly.

I don't know how to congratulate the missionary even today. I always visit him and thank him very much for what he did for me.

Philip Muinde, 16, Kenya

Philip, with friends at Joytown, Kenya.

My name is Santi Rakshart. I was born on the 1st January 1965 at Udon Thani Hospital. I have been handicapped in my right leg since I was born. My parents never came to see me while I was at the hospital, and I lived in the hospital, looked after by doctors, until I was nine years old. Then I escaped from the hospital because I wanted to see the fair at Tung Srimeong, Udorn Province. I walked from 10 o'clock at night until the morning. I didn't dare come back to the hospital because I thought I would be punished. So I decided to run away from

Udorn to escape punishment. I went by bus to Korn Kan Province in the morning. I was very hungry. I cried. Suddenly I saw the temple not far from here and went there. I had a breakfast and lunch from the monk and in the evening I tried to earn my living by selling newspapers. I bought food and a new shirt and trousers. I lived in Korn Kan about one month, playing near the school because I wanted to learn, very much. I saw many pupils and thought 'Why didn't I have a chance to learn like the others?' Sometimes I cried and looked upset. I had trouble from the boys that lived in the temple. I couldn't fight them because I was handicapped. I tried to ask them not to beat me like that but they still did not stop. They always hid my braces while I went to eat. That made it difficult to walk. I couldn't bear it so I escaped from them to go to Maha Sarakham Province. And again I tried to find a temple and shelter. This time I asked the monk to teach me to read and write like the others and he agreed. He loved me so much with my ambitions, I learnt and passed my exams. Later I travelled in many parts of Thailand. I lived in the East for about a year, and went to Bangkok and Chachoengsao. At Chachoengsao I lived in the market and the railway station. I slept in the day, but in the night I sold newspapers to earn my living. I had enough money to hire a room, and used my room as much as possible to learn by myself. If I couldn't understand, I would go to ask the teacher that lived nearby. And so in my travels I came from Padrene to Chon Buri and Pattaya, where there was a school which I went to. I always remembered what they taught and tried to collect money to buy books. I was very interested in the English language and tried to understand it. I liked to travel and see everything that gave me an experience until my age was 13. Then I thought I couldn't spend my life like this. So I went to Bangkok where I had been told there was a Department of Public Welfare which had a home for crippled children. And finally I requested help to enter this home. I stayed there for a while, but then I escaped once again in the night at one o'clock because I was hurt by the older boys. I travelled to the north and went to the elephant fair at Surin Province. I slept at the railway station and was arrested by the police and accused of madness and was sent to the Eastern Reception Home for Boys. Finally I was sent to the Home for the crippled children again. I thought that I wouldn't escape again because I would have no future for myself. It was a dark and endless way ahead. I tried to tolerate as much as I could. My teachers spoke gently and urged me to be tolerant for my own sake. I love them.

The best way I can thank all of them is to try and learn and to be a good boy, speak so truly and be punctual. And my motto is to do a good thing and never to be in error.

Santi Rakshart, 15, Thailand

73

Adolescence and young love

Apart from difficulties with my eyes, I dare to say that our two worlds are identical. I have the same tastes, the same ideas and above all the same mentality as any adolescent. I come across the same difficult periods as the majority of girls of my age. In the emotional sphere, I experience almost the same sentimental problems and experience at least the same emotional problems as them in overcoming certain worries and problems.

In fact, in what way do I differ from others, if it is not the opinion and the 'picture' that others have of me? So I am a young girl like others, a young girl who loves to live and who follows an ideal. Why do people continue to treat me and consider me as different, indeed as abnormal . . .

Alice Renaud, 17

One day I fell in love with a girl who was not deaf and was one of Marcelo's friends. As I could not speak with her my good friend, Marcelo, explained to her how she should speak to me. She accepted it. I asked her to be my girlfriend. She liked me but her mother did not want her to have a deaf boyfriend. I suffered a lot. Fortunately my brother helped me and explained to me lots of things I did not understand.

Now I only have deaf friends.

Carlos Gunther, 18

I miss just simply being able to walk out of the door, shouting to my mum "Ta-ra, I'm just going to town, won't be long". Now it's all strict organisation, you feel like a famous film star, with all the bodyguards. First I have to find someone that can drive me by car to my destination (knowing of course that he can lift me). Then I have to take a female with me to help me to the toilet. I make sure there is enough money in my purse for a taxi in case I can't get a lift back.

The indignities of being handicapped get to be a bit much for me, for instance, when you go out somewhere posh and you have to have someone to go into the toilets with you.

After being in a chair three years it would be a lie to say I wouldn't prefer to walk, but my future looks a hell of a lot brighter, and I will say I have experienced and enjoyed things normal kids will never appreciate.

Sandra Gaskell

My feelings are hurt by people who treat me as a freak. I like pop music, books and swimming, and all the things that teenagers like doing. The only thing that is different about me is I don't see as well as other people.

Kristina Brown, 16

74

Love is a strange thing.
It seems to take away all your reason.
You seem to forget to do
What is good for you.
All that I can say is that I love you.
Sure, before, I vowed to love you always,
But though I do, that doesn't make me an object
That you have the right to play with.
Even though I want to hurt you like I have been hurt,
My heart wouldn't let me.

Halina Dudzic, 18

Halina is from Canada. She was a high school student going into grade twelve when she sustained a near-fatal injury in a car accident. She has lost her speech completely. She is also confined to a wheelchair and is having great difficulty in writing, but uses a typewriter.

Danuta Gieraktowska, 16

75

Towards independence

At home, I have no one to spend my time with. All the kids of my age like to be with me, but my mother keeps telling me, "No, You don't know your own limits. I'm far too afraid that something will happen to you." Then she wonders why no one visits me. She really is far too terrified, she mistrusts everyone far too much, and is far too worried about me. Because of her attitude, here I am reduced to keeping little kids amused or to being alone the whole time.

Anonymous, partially sighted

I am a normal person with a sight problem. I am not spoiled at home because of my problem. I have to do my share of work but where my problem may cause danger, eg driving, I am not expected or allowed to play a part. I have been brought up to be independent and I want to be that way. Where I need help I most certainly accept it but where people say, "Oh, you can't do that because of your sight", I get annoyed. The type of help which I accept is; having things explained which I can't see, sometimes being shown what to do and having some signs read to me.

Maryanne Mannen, 15

When I was younger my mum's aim was to make me as independent as possible and although my mum and I had many a row I now realise that it was for my own good. But I know quite a few children who have taken part in what's called an "independence course". The child goes away from home for about a week to ten days and is taught how to cook, wash his own clothes and so on. But in my view it is pointless sending a child on an independence course if, when the child goes home, he is waited on hand and foot by his parents.

Andrew Butterworth, 16

I think my idea of a full life is that I would like to do as many things as I could do and what I wanted to without people telling me what I can and can't do. I think that it is important, especially as you get older you must learn to be independent, to do things for yourself.

Sue Logan, 18

It is sometimes very rough being crippled. Some people treat us like we're helpless people, and often do not know our capabilities. They would be very surprised at what we can do for ourselves.

Jeff Young, 18

Usually when I want help nobody comes, but sometimes when I am trying to be independent, half a dozen people arrive to help.

Haider Tirmizey, 15

They wouldn't let me carry a plate. I was still wearing a bib. At seven! At eleven I was still pretty helpless. You can't expect people to start knowing how to dress at eleven when they've been brought up to be helpless.
Later, I went to a special boarding school for handicapped children. There were only a couple of helpers to about fifty people, so you had to do things for yourself. There was a marvellous matron too. When you asked her to do something, she'd say 'do it yourself'. It was a real shock, but you did.
But then the school developed. There were three resident doctors, a sick bay, two helpers to every child. I know they've brought in many more severely disabled people, but there are also some who would previously have got a glass of water themselves. Now they ask someone.   *David Ruebain, 17*

I like to get people helping me sometimes, but not all the time. I want to try to do it myself first and if I can't do it, I call and if I can do it I just do it, without even calling "Mom".
I try my best to work as hard as I can. I think I can do it mostly, but if I have trouble my Mom or Dad helps me, like reaching something on my dresser. First they have to see me try to do it.   *Jordy Davis, 9*

Some handicapped people can quite easily deceive other people, who are new to them, in doing what they ought to do themselves, like pushing them in a wheelchair or help them to stand up.   *Haider Tirmizey, 15*

Mark Jones

We're not dumb

The worst thing about my problem is the fact that people who are not partially sighted are under the impression that I am an idiot. Just because of my short sightedness they think I am less intelligent than they are.

I am left out of conversations involving political matters, literature or art as they seem to think I don't understand such things. This is very degrading for me and does little for my morale.

Kristina Brown, 16

Some people's attitudes towards disabled and handicapped people are appalling. People in wheelchairs are no different from anyone else. All that is different is that when they were born the brain may have been slightly damaged, and as a result their legs or arms will not work properly. These people who are unfortunate enough to have been born like this, are quite capable of doing almost anything, just like anyone else.

Anyone in this world who thinks that all people in wheelchairs, or people who walk strangely are stupid or mentally backward do not realise how inconsiderate and foolish they are. I feel very angry when I see people making stupid remarks about the disabled. In fact the disabled are just as capable of going to university. They can achieve fantastic results in all subjects, they can swim and win sports trophies, and play musical instruments perfectly well.

People from this school are victims, in some cases, of very serious disabilities. Despite the fact they are handicapped they regard their life as normal, after all it is normal!

A good example at the school is Panos who is Greek and very seriously handicapped. His eyesight is poor, he is confined to a wheelchair, cannot speak to a normal standard, is unable to feed himself without assistance and cannot push his own chair. When he first came to the school he could not speak English but despite his serious speaking difficulties he learnt to speak English fluently in one year. This is an extremely good example of how people can overcome difficulties.

I hope that one day very soon, people will come to realise that the handicapped are not objects to stare at or be pitied. They are just human beings.

Paul Smith, 14

The people who attend our school are not as unintelligent as many people think. We hate people who make remarks about us because they have not taken the trouble to meet us and get to know us. It makes me very cross when people say we are stupid. At our school we all have problems but *we* don't go round making fun of each other.

Allan Robinson, 16

This is a mouth drawing by Šárka Sýkorová

So what if I'm awkward,
always wiggling and shaking.
So what if I'm clumsy,
always dropping and breaking.

So what if you have trouble
understanding what I'm trying to say.
Does that mean I'm dumb?
NO WAY.

Heidi Janz, 14

Wong Sai Ming

I don't want your pity
And I don't want your help
I just want a fair chance
And acceptance as myself
I know I'm not the same as you

Chrissie Chadwick

80

We have certain rights

What I need from you is only my rights and not a lot of sympathy.

Mutinda Kimilu, 9

Everybody has a right to do what they want, and to do it when they want to. We do not need pity; we do not need to be soft-soaped all the time. We are all just as good at doing things — we can do everything everyone else does. We are equal and we want to be treated as equals, like human beings. We are not dumb; we are just as clever as anyone else. We should have the right to work.

Lee Garrett, 13

The handicapped have all the rights in the world to lead a full and active life.
Our goals are to try the best we can.
We all have the right to do what we choose to do.
The world is hard for all including me.
So let's make the best of it to our full potential.

Alastair Whitefield

My name is Joanna Summers. I am thirteen and partially sighted and — may I add — a human being. I am practically normal, so why do people treat me like an idiot? I am not implying communism. But equality is important to the "handicapped". It creates an us-and-them situation which would be damaging if "we" were a strong enough movement to fight back. In fact, society picks on the weakest members.
I know it is a case of survival of the fittest, and that is right in a kind of way, but everyone has the right, or should have, to have a decent chance! I feel a certain hatred against society, a hatred that society manufacturers.

Joanna Summers, 13

The Rights and Needs of Handicapped People
They need to be helped.
They need to be loved by others.
They need to be respected.
They need to be considered.
They need to be educated.
They need to be trusted.
They need to be appreciated as useful people.
They need to lead a good, happy life.
They need to be fed.

Mwaniki Makau, 10

Keep your pity for animals

Apart from the annoying factor of breaking things, one of the worst things for me is being treated like a baby. You know the sort of thing I mean, "Hello dear, how are you? Would you like a sweetie? Aren't you cute?" It's bad enough for other handicapped children I know, but at least they are full sized.

Sophie Partridge, 11

It's not the handicapped people who need rehabilitating but the rest of the world. Don't pat on the head, offer help, talk to handicapped people out of pity. Talk to them because you like them. Otherwise don't bother.

David Ruebain, 17

I stayed at home until I was four. When I was playing in the garden, my neighbouring child saw me and ran away, saying, "Strange girl!" Some visitors to my house said, "Poor girl!" I couldn't understand why they said so. Once I asked my mother, "Why do people say, 'Strange girl' or 'Poor girl!'?" She wouldn't answer, with her head down and a sad expression on her face. Since then I have seldom gone out of my house. *Kimie Yoshida*

The handicapped — what do we stand for in the eyes of the world? Imbeciles? Garbage?
The answer could be concluded from the strange stare that is cast on us. Certainly it is not full of disgust, but pity and sorrow. Should we not be grateful? No, because we do not want to be treated with sympathy and privilege, but to be looked upon just as one of them. *Chan Wai Sang, 18*

In my experience people are very frightened of me. They don't know how to act when they are with me. They either ignore me or treat me as if I am a baby. *Jacqueline Reed, 16*

Sometimes I envy those who can go to restaurants and can feed themselves while I have to depend on others to feed me. I also notice people often stare at me, or have a pitiful look on their faces. Personally I don't like people taking pity on me when I am no different from anyone else.   *Cathy Katon, 17*

I hate people who feel sorry for me, because I don't feel a bit sorry for myself.
                                        Viviana Ortolan, 18

I see through your eyes pity for me
I don't want your pity or your lies
You see my chair instead of me
You see many things wrong with me
    instead of just me.
                        Colleen Henley

I don't have any real friends. These people pity me and call themselves my friends but I don't even know who they are. Even if I knew them I wouldn't call them friends because real friends don't pity each other; they understand each other. Do you understand me? People, be my friends and don't pity me.

Swati Kothari

Lumping us together

I am not my disability, I'm me. I have dyslexia and I've had polio, but I'm not 'a dyslexic' or 'a cripple', I'm me.

John Swan, 14

Adults who look after people who have the same illness, the same handicap, cannot understand, will never understand that they are all different.

We ourselves, what we want to say first of all to the adults who look after us, is that we are forty-eight different personalities. There is no such personality as a muscular dystrophic. Indeed, I have muscular dystrophy, with all the characteristics of muscular dystrophy, but I am a person — François, Bruno, Thierry, Gildas . . .

We are above all ourselves, before becoming sufferers of muscular dystrophy; we are individuals with different characters.

Just as well, otherwise one would get annoyed; it would be boring; you couldn't learn things, and become absorbed in them.

Here, one sometimes has the impression of no longer having any personality. If I am not regarded as my own self, well then it is not easy to be oneself.

By a group of children from France

When many of us go out visiting at the same time, it's called a "dove-release" from our institution. And most of us have difficulty breaking out of the safety that such a group gives. This means we rarely get to know anybody outside the institution. Linde has become our world.

But the non-disabled have their own handicap, too; the insecurity towards someone different from themselves. These "different" people don't need to be handicapped. They can be other minority groups — foreign workers, Lapps, and others who cause people to turn and look at them in the street. This can seem frightening or threatening, but it can also cause curiosity which in fact doesn't need to be negative.

But the insecurity can appear in negative ways: mobbing, infantile treatment, selfishness, intolerance. It's also likely that non-disabled get afraid of us because of the noisy and scolding way we behave. But this might be because since we can't claim ourselves physically, the mouth is the only tool most of us can use.

By a school group from Norway

Life, of course, could be easier for the handicapped if they were more widely accepted in the community as being actual people, not, as is so often the case as incapable, alienated specimens. The majority are normal people and detest the word 'handicapped' since it immediately classifies them to society as just being organisms. This, in turn, creates disillusionment, resentment, bitterness, insecurity and, above all, embarrassment.

The label is a diminishing factor — it upsets, it degrades.

Velma Sylvan, 16

84

The mass media could do more. It's O.K. to let the disabled participate in presentation-programmes about the disabled, but how often do we see the disabled in other programmes? With the disabled only presented in programmes about themselves we reinforce the prejudice about the disabled as a special group. *By a group of physically handicapped children*

I don't want your pity. You think that just because we have a problem with our vision that we can't do things for ourselves, but we all are equal. And why did they give the title 'handicap'? Do you know how offensive that is. You could make people want to die or even want to kill. We don't want to be left out. *Mauree Hughes, 13*

Mauree

We wish that certain projects put forward by the centre were done so without any ulterior motives. When we saw that leaflet they were circulating about holidays being therapeutic we were furious. We all consider ourselves as adolescents who are alive and well and who only travel in order to see what a country is like! *Anonymous*

My ambition is to get out and work somewhere with people who aren't disabled, but I don't know if I could. I will still try. I want to be recognised for what I am — Viviana Ortolan. *Viviana Ortolan*

My first school was a local place for handicapped children, two to seven. They put bibs on you and made you sing 'We shall overcome'. Pathetic! At the time they were mixing mentally subnormal with physically handicapped kids.
If you are born handicapped you are labelled from birth. You are sent to special schools, special clubs, special holiday centres. You mix only with other handicapped people. You end up believing you are a lot more handicapped than you are. *David Ruebain, 17*

you see my handicape first and me last.

Colleen Henley, 17

It could be you

One afternoon as I was going down the street a little boy walked up and started to make fun of me. I didn't say anything because I knew he didn't understand my disease, so I just went home. About three days later the little boy who made fun of me got struck by a car. He got hurt bad and is now crippled for life. I bet he won't make fun of me anymore because he won't like it if anyone makes fun of him. Now that little boy and I are friends and have a good time together.

Lisa Bouchard, 11

It isn't fair to hear perfectly healthy people scorn others for their misfortune. After all, they are the lucky ones. If the lucky ones were in those unfortunate people's position, they would soon stop laughing. *Patricia Flynn, 16*

When I found that I could not walk or feel my legs, I felt frightened and wondered what was happening to me. This happened on May the 12th 1979. It felt like I had no legs. I spent a lot of time in hospital that year. I went to hospital and learnt to do things for myself.
Well what happened to me was that I had a burst blood vessel or a pinched nerve in the spine. The doctors do not know if I will walk again.
My fear is that I will not be accepted as who I am, but as someone in a wheelchair. *Lynda Burch, 14*

I am an eighteen-year-old epileptic girl. Why I am writing about myself is because of my disability. I felt there was no future in my existence and was always so sad and depressed.
However, with this epilepsy I am very fortunate to be able to get out and do things for myself. Little did I know that there is somewhere someone much worse off than myself. I joined a group where three people have only one leg — another six are blind etc. and to see this sure does make me stop feeling sorry for myself.
Not long ago we all went away for a holiday to a skiing resort. When we arrived back from the mountain I would walk into the front room where I would see and hear a warm friendly voice saying "Hello" then call me by my name and ask if I would like a cup of coffee. The blind boy would then stand up and get it for me. I was amazed that he knew where to go. We chatted and found that we both had the same interests. I love writing short stories and poetry and I found he liked the same.
At last I have found happiness and but one prayer to be answered. That he will see. *Rosemary Munoz, 18*

One minute happy — the next handicapped.   *Marc Tomczak*

Respect before help

Help Us By Respecting Us

I warn you, first of all, this is not a story of my life. It is also not a fantasized yarn about what I'd like to be. It isn't a sad story about my physically disabled condition. No way am I going to use a sob story for a person's entertainment or understanding. This . . . is the story of the public and their stereotype that they give us, the people in wheelchairs. So stand by to read about yourself. Stereotyping is a daily exercise. It particularly bothers people like us. For example, just before last Christmas, I was waiting for a friend in a shopping mall. I was guarding my friend's shopping bag, when a small child tried to grab the bag. I asked the child to leave it alone, and just then, the mother arrived on the spot. Calling the child's name, she said "Leave the boy alone", and looking at me said, "poor little boy".

This is about the worst remark I have ever heard. It has also brought an important point. Handicapped people are anything but poor little boys and girls. We are not depressed. We are not in pain. We don't like people who tell us that we are helpless little human beings, because we're not. This is what the public must remember. People who stare are people who care? Maybe, but when I go into town, I feel like an alien being. When little kids stare, that is natural. But when people over eighteen just stand and gape, it disgusts you. Once when I was about seven or so, my brother was pushing my wheelchair around the Domain. Suddenly, an old couple caught sight of us. Wherever we went, they went, staring. Eventually, my brother, who was three years older than me at the time, asked them if they would like a photograph as it lasts a lot longer. See? People who stare are a pain in the neck. There are other things. For example,

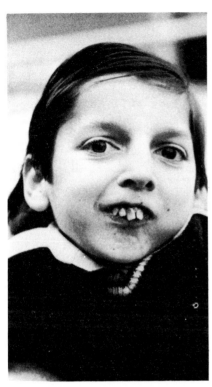

talking to the person I'm with, rather than myself. Treating us like kids when we're teenagers. Discrimination. Every little thing that sets us apart from normal people. The big point also is that physically handicapped and mentally handicapped are two different people: one is either in a wheelchair, or has lack of co-ordination, the other has a mental problem. So, remember these points.
I certainly hope this affects you, the public. It would make life easier if we had this respect. Sure, we need help. But people can be over-helpful sometimes. We, the people in wheelchairs, lead normal lives of work and recreation.
As for myself, I am fourteen years old, and I am a fifth former with School Certificate English. This year, I am trying for School Certificate History and Art. My recreations are listening to Rock and New Wave music, watching television, going to movies, concerts etc. I hope to review Rock and New Wave music in the future.
Now, are you wiser?

Andrew Bhana, 14

Helping is an art

The most important thing for me is to do things by myself. Sometimes I am doing something like taking off my jumper and someone says, 'Let me take it off for you'. I say no. I want to do it myself. I like to be asked.

Viviana Ortolan, 18

People don't need to worry about not helping. It's not necessary to help a handicapped person in the street because a severely handicapped will not be there. And they really have developed their own ways of coping — otherwise they wouldn't be there on their own. So ask them if they need help. But not if they're coping quite well and getting on by themselves. Always ask them and listen when they say 'no'. Don't pay a second thought really.

David Ruebain

I feel happy when people who don't know me say hello. That might not mean much to others, but to me it does, because some people don't even say hello. It makes me feel happy because they know that I am a person.

Viviana Ortolan

If I was asked to give other people some tips about how to help a handicapped, I would say that it should be to think thoroughly before you ask a handicapped person a question. I am sure that somebody would get very offended by me being so rude, but don't you be that. For instead of just babbling along to the seeing companion about me, he could ask me. And secondly there is no reason to keep standing on the other side of the street and yelling: "Now you can cross", when you, the seeing one, are able to see that I am going to cross.

Kim Preuthun

How NOT to Help

According to me the worst mistakes that people
make are:
When they help and praise themselves.
When they help by giving things that are useless and they want to get rid of them.
When they help, but keep looking keenly at my handicap.
When they help, but keep asking me many questions about my handicap.
When they help me sarcastically.
When they help unwillingly.
When they help, but keep abusing at the same time.
When they help without love.
When they help me as somebody useless.

Mwaniki Makau, 10

90

A TOUS LES ENFANTS
DU MONDE. JE SUIS
DANS UNE ECOLE
POUR AVEUGLES. JE
DEMANDE AUX ENFANTS
QUI VOIENT D'AIDER LES
ENFANTS AVEUGLES.

To all the children in the world: I go to a school for blind children. I ask all children who can see to help blind children.

Chantal Nicole, 7

We're no heroes

The whole thing about being handicapped is overrated. It's just as if the whole world all had five legs. We'd look back and wonder how people had coped with only two legs. We might say, 'My God, how could he walk with only two legs. It must be dreadfully tiring!'

Most people who've been born handicapped get used to it. They don't know anything else and on a purely practical level they get over their disadvantages — often because other people do the housework or fetch the shopping or drive them to school or whatever.

And to a certain degree they are at an advantage. I mean I get into the cinema free and I always get a bigger portion of chips when I eat out.

Who else has gone to Lourdes, and Bologna and over Europe in the last two years?

People will make allowances for you if you're late so you can lead a much freer life. If I miss a day at school I just have to say I fell down. At my old school we used to go into town and if you didn't have any money you just used to look handicapped and people would come and give you cash just like that. So if we hadn't got any money we thought, let's go out and get some money. We'd just have a sad dog face and look miserable.

The reasons lie basically with prejudices so they're not real benefits, but they're there because of the misconceptions people have about handicapped people and if we had Utopia there wouldn't be the prejudice and people would realise that a handicapped person is not special.

Whether you're handicapped or not you spend your life trying to do as much to make yourself happy as possible. If a handicapped person decides what he wants to do, basically he'll do that because it's very important to him. If he's got the motivation — and a lot of the motivation is taken out by other people, unfortunately — he can do what he wants to do.

It's what you are and what you make of it that matters. And so, for somebody with no arms and no legs, it's not traumatic for him to do something, for him to get up in the morning and go to work because that's what he has to do.

I'd make an exception with people who become handicapped because they've known different and I really can't speak for them, but everybody is what they're born with. So getting dressed in the morning, say, might take a bit longer for me, but I have to do it and so it's not something I think 'Oh God, I've got to be brave because I've got to get dressed now.' It's just a part of you.

It's all greatly overrated is what I'm trying to say. It's certainly there, but I think it's overrated and it's created by other people. Some handicapped people, because they're told they're handicapped, genuinely believe that they are, and so getting up in the morning really does become a task. It becomes something that they genuinely believe is difficult for them to do, not because they have found it so, but because people have told them so.

It's not their fault, it's the fault of people who segregate people into handicapped clubs, schools, handicapped centres, handicapped everything.

If you're born with one arm, for example, you are not born with the belief that you are a lesser person or that you can't sail a boat because you've only got one arm. That belief is bestowed upon you by other people who tell you so right from when you're a baby . . . when you are not allowed to get your own glass of milk, when you are told that you can't do it, so let other people do it. It's from the very, very start and it takes many subtle forms. People talk down to you, rather than at you, you're talked about by everyone. 'What shall we do with him tomorrow?' in front of you. 'What's the best thing to do for him?' You genuinely believe that you are not as much of a person as somebody else. But that's not where the emphasis lies. The emphasis is that you are a disabled person in all senses of the word. Not only physically but socially disabled and so you won't be able to cope without our assistance, so you must mix with other disabled people. You're inadequate. They never tell you you're inadequate, but that's what fundamentally you begin to believe. Everybody is always telling you how sad it is and you just come to believe you're almost a second class person. So you expect people to dress you, and you will never be able to do it yourself. You would never think of having a say in your life.

And everybody pities you when you may not need it. I used to go to primary school by taxi everyday. It was not a disabled school, but the council decided I needed a taxi and I used to get bought an ice cream by the taxi driver everyday. At that time I expected it from people, which is what was so awful. I expected it because I was 'handicapped' and 'under-privileged'. I believed I was going through a dreadful experience although I couldn't actually put my finger on anything being dreadful. There's no excuse for pity whatsoever. None at all. It's totally negative and totally destructive. It's bad for the individual who's doing it and it's bad for the person they're doing it to. It just doesn't have a need, it's bad, it's immoral. The only purpose it serves is increasing the person's belief that he's an object of pity and not an individual.

My boarding school produced a film called 'Where There's A Will', and it showed all the marvellous things: 'Last year our boys won this canoe race. Isn't that wonderful.' It was the most pathetic canoe race ever. It had no meaning whatsoever. 'Look at these people with crutches, they can climb a mountain.' The only one aim in that is for everybody to think 'Gasp, Gasp, how wonderful.' There was this element of sort of like making us like heroes.

So I thought, well I'll go to an ordinary school, and I'll impress them all with my ability to dress myself and the rest of it. And I came here and I was stunned by how much more mature they were as people, because I was acting like maybe a twelve year old.

You suddenly realise that you're just another person, no more special.

David Ruebain

Problems galore

Handicapped people have got so many problems which are more than a pen can write.

Samuel Kinyanjui

Considering physical limitations, discomfort and everything else, it may be surprising that we, the handicapped, don't suffer mental and nervous breakdowns as well. We have to be stronger than so-called normal people.

Jacqueline Reed, 16

When I became a disabled child I spent so many years being taken to different hospitals for treatment and all these years my age mates were still proceeding with education. I came to start learning when my age mates were six years ahead of me.

Samuel Kinyanjui

Like most of the children at my school I have more time off from school than the average, then one thing leads to another and we fall behind with our work. This means we have to work ten times as hard and be ten times as good at the end. *Adrian Allen, 14*

EDITOR'S NOTE: Some disabled children obviously have a bucketful of problems like pain, family rejection, boredom or delayed schooling. But there is one problem that did not come across very strongly in the entries the children wrote — perhaps for obvious reasons of reticence — and that is the problem of going to the toilet.
Some of the children spoke to me about this at length in individual interviews, and it is an area of major difficulty.
At schools for the physically disabled, for instance, a large number of staff are needed just to help children in wheelchairs onto the toilet, and to deal with the problems of soiled clothing. Within the family, there are the same physical problems. And as the children grow older, it becomes harder and harder to lift them.
Remember, too, that people in wheelchairs can never go out unless they can be sure of getting to toilets that have wide enough doors for wheelchairs. They can be completely housebound just because there are no suitable toilets in libraries, schools, cinemas, shops or discos. Then comes the problem of making friends and later of dating. If you cannot go to the toilet on your own can you imagine being on your first date and asking your date to take you to the toilet? It's quite a stopper.

Did you know that I am a spina bifida and when I was first born I became very very sick. Ever since then I've been in hospital a lot of times — more than half of my life. I get fed up in hospital but nobody listens.
I wash by myself. I have a bath with a guard on it and a nurse is somewhere near. But I can't pass a motion on my own — I have to have a 'bag'. I'd like to be 'my own self'. By being my own self I mean not having a bag. So I want doctors to help children not to have spina bifida and not to have disposable bags. I'd be able to do more things if I'd been 'my own self'.
I can't manage without someone to help now, but I can see that I could handle my own money in the future, and choose my clothes. I would still like a companion for safety.

Grant Brosnan, 13

Lots of disabled people would like to play certain musical instruments, but they can't and if they wanted to be in an orchestra they probably wouldn't be able to, because if they were in a wheelchair more than likely they would be called a fire hazard.

Bernadette Hagan, 13

One of the quite large problems is that we have to drink a lot and it seems to me that either the parents don't realise this and therefore don't push their kids very much. Later my teacher told me that a schoolfriend of mine had died from kidney trouble.

Andrew Butterworth, 16

When I want the toilet and tell a nurse they often say, 'In a minute' — but they come back fifteen minutes later!

Stuart, 14

Marcelo Pereyra

Problems: getting out and about

It is not much fun in the winter because I cannot get outside as much because my wheelchair cannot move very easily and I might get frostbite.

Jonathon Marsh, 9

I can remember when I was not in a wheelchair. It's sort of difficult to forget. I get kind of sick being pushed around in a wheelchair because I have to go where people push me whether I want to or not.

Sean Hagan

There are many things that make it difficult for a person in a wheelchair to shop. The first is the difficulty of getting there, because pavements are so difficult to get up and down and the roads through the town centre are the busiest. If you get there many shops have a step to the door or are too small for a wheelchair to get around. In some department stores there is no step and plenty of room, but you can't get through the check-out!

David Garnett

If I was in charge of the world I would like to see more ramps — not steps everywhere. All houses to have wide doors and large bedrooms, and motorcars to have sliding doors and to always have a nurse to assist Mom. Make telephones lower. More space in 'loos' and more toilet chairs and a better school van.

Mark Fitzgerald, 16

My name is Sue Pearce and I was born with spina bifida. I think my sister feels upset because I cannot go out with her more often. The most aggravating thing was when I first went to the swimming pool. When I got there, there were about twenty steps to go up. And my sister paid to get in and it was a lot of money for me and my sister. I never had my swim because I was unable to walk up the stairs.

Susan Pearce, 13

To be disabled is not very nice because you can't get about like other children. When I go out I need somebody with me just in case I should fall.

Kevin Dowling

I would like to go to the shop for my mom but I can't because the pavement is too high.

Joyce Kirkwood, 15

Dear Politician
I am writing to complain about the space in the toilets and shops. I think it is disgraceful and I wish you would do something about it.

Debbie Parker, 12

It gets kind of boring to sit in a wheelchair all day long.

Joyce Kirkwood, 15

I think that it should be law that all new shops that are being built, should *Wong Sai Ming* have facilities for the disabled, because there aren't just the odd hundred or so, there are thousands of disabled people in every country. It isn't too much to ask, is it? All I am asking for are some decent lifts, some ramps and quite a reasonable amount of room to park our cars. *Carol Jones, 15*

People at cinemas should be nicer. When I went to a cinema the people at the door were rude. My sister asked if the picture was downstairs and the lady turned around and said that there was no room for me in my wheelchair. She said it in a really horrible way. I wouldn't have minded if it had been said in a nice way or if the lady had apoiogised. They should have cinemas where they have special places where wheelchairs can go. *Peter McFiggins, 13*

97

Helping people in wheelchairs

Important buildings and big shops should have electronic doors, ramps and lifts.

Stuart Burnett, 14

Dear MP,

I hate the way the council treat the disabled. When you are out and looking for a WC you rarely see a sign that means that the WC is equipped to help disabled people.
I want to be independent. Besides, I won't always have someone to push me about all my life so if you want to help disabled people get on in life, I ask you to press the local authorities to think about us the next time they build a public place.

John Brown, 15

When a disabled person is going into a public place like a library and they can't get the doors opened, people should help them and not stand around and stare or gawk.

Douglas Roper

If I was in charge of the world I would change a great deal of things and introduce new ideas. I would have a ticket made like a season ticket for a train, only this ticket would allow a disabled person to get in any club, cinema or sports event without being refused.
All the bus companies would have to make the buses with a smaller step, so the conductor or a friend can help the person who is in a wheelchair to get into the bus. There will be spaces for a wheelchair to park next to a seat.
I would have all the councils of the world put in small curbs in each road and also two car ramps, so that a person who cannot go up or down a curb can use the car ramps.
The rail companies would have to make wider doors on trains and wider corridors. The councils would have to build the public toilets a lot wider and without a step at the door.
If I was in charge of the world I would get all these things done.

Michael Santoro, 15

If a handicapped person is in difficulty, such as crossing a road, ask if they need help. If they say no you must take that for an answer.

When helping a wheelchair down a kerb your foot on one of the foot bars and hold on to the handle bars with both hands and pull.

Anyone in a wheelchair needing to make a very urgent phone call can't do so because the door is too stiff and the phone boxes are too small and some have a very steep step.

When a person is in calipers and is in need of help going down the kerb, just get hold of a metal bar across their back and lift.

Asra Jilani, 12

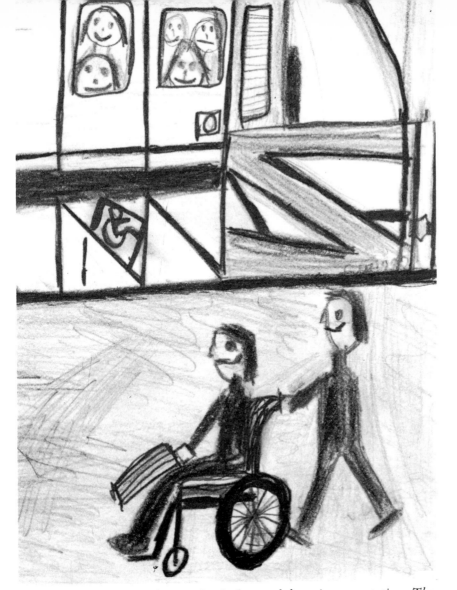

I wish there was not a step between the platform and the train on our stations. The train I draw would be ideal for me.   *Urs Häfeli, 14*

EDITOR'S NOTE: *Pushing a wheelchair sounds easy, but you can easily tip the person out. Disabled people can also find it very painful to be taken over bumpy ground, or suddenly dropped down kerbs. When you lower a person down a kerb, tilt the wheelchair backwards slightly, put your feet on the tipping lever at the back, and as you lower the wheelchair down on to the street arch your back and bend your knees to take the weight of the wheelchair. It is essential that both wheels hit the road at the same time.*

Don't attempt stairs unless you have two fairly strong people. And a small point: never pull at the arm rests, because they can come out if you do.

About being spastic

Janina

I was born a spastic but my parents did not know until I was two when they noticed my head was always moving in all directions with no control at all. I was taken to doctors and was examined. My parents were then told I was a spastic. At the time they were asked if they would be able to cope with me as there was a special hostel where I could be placed. But their decision to keep me at home makes me realize today that they both loved and sacrificed a lot of me. My childhood was very happy.

I have a speech difficulty and at times during the years of growing up I was constantly frustrated because no one understood what I was trying to say to them. So eventually I made up my mind to talk ONLY with my family and friends. My one immediate fear in those days was to go out for a walk down the street by myself, because people would stop and *stare* at me as if I came from another planet, which made me wonder *am I different from them*.

As I grew older my life evolved more and more around my family. We went out quite often on day trips and my father taught me to ignore all those "stupid people" who would laugh and jeer at me.

Janina Smietanka

I was born with cerebral palsy so I'll never walk. I'm nearly always in a wheelchair. I have a lot of trouble eating and I talk real funny. People look at me because I keep wriggling. I also have to wear a back brace because my spine is bent and I can't sit up without my brace. My worst thing is I can't go to the toilet by myself.

My trouble is that my muscles are weak and don't work together like other people's. And especially when I'm excited or nervous they keep moving.

Luckily I have a machine to help me write and with help I'm going to get through school. I'm getting good grades but I started late so I'm working extra hard and doing three years work in two years.

Janey Stevenson

EDITOR'S NOTE: *Spasticity is also known as cerebral palsy.*

Most spastic people are born with perfect muscles and perfect bodies. But parts of their brain are damaged so that the muscles don't receive the right messages. This means that they don't have proper control over movement.

Spastic people can have <u>no</u> movement or <u>constant</u> movement or movement that is <u>shaky or jerky</u>. Some people can do nothing for themselves while others may have just a slight problem with walking, writing or speech. In short no two people are exactly the same because the damage to the brain differs. Provided other parts of the brain aren't damaged spastic children are as intelligent as everyone else.

Spasticity is not hereditary — it is often caused by complications at birth, such as lack of oxygen. German measles during the early months of pregnancy is also a cause.

Maria João Miranda Escravana, 10

David Heckendorf, 14

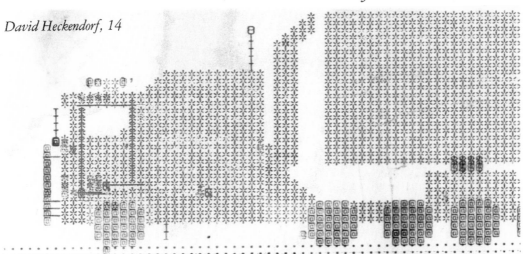

Spastic children often cannot draw easily because they cannot control the movement of their pen or pencil. They could easily have been deterred by the problems of contributing drawings to a book like this. Nonetheless a great many spastic children sent me their pictures. Maria (above) spent hours on her drawing and David (bottom picture) got round the problem by doing his drawing on a typewriter.

About dyslexia

My name is Ian and I am Dislesic and theas bad things about it. When teched at school right in my book whoch your spelling your hand riting is scruff. When some people say you are thick as two planck of wood or you speell like a 6 year olled. When I see a good book I look in side it and if the words are to harred I haff to put it back. If a littall boy or girl comes up to hows about 4 to 9 and cums up and says what dus that say and I do not no I feel that I won't to criy. I do not like to say I do not no and then they laff at me. That is the west thing I hatte about beeing Dislesic.

The things I like about been Dislesic is that I no I can get good help from the instutute and they never poot whoch your spelling. I like every one that gose to the instutute speshelly Mrs Conalley because she is my teacher and they are all cinde to us at the instutute. No one can say you are thick because you are all about the same. The teches are good to you because some of there suns and dorters is Dislesic.

Ian Davies, 15

When i was at school at first i tried to make out I could read and write to the teachers and friends. i used to find excuses for not reading out loud i would say i had a sore throat. i would write badly so that the teacher couldn't tell if I had spelt things wrong. In maths I could do the sums if I could read questions. Now if i have to fill a form in i say i have a bad hand or i haven't got my glasses.

Lynda Royle

When I was five I found techers could not read my work. They were nagging on every peace of work. They put See me! on every peace of work. I would have to go out to the class then the teacher would say look at this rubbish. I felt like iting the teacher, but something just stop me. She would keep going on at me. She said "Why are your p and b all the ronge way round". I just didn't no why. It felt like neglechted. Nobody cared.
Just no body.
I saw the T.V. program on dyslexie. They were getting the same problem as me. Then after it I said to my mom if I have that I will be free. Now I have noun I have had it four months. Things have changed. I am just like a normal person but some days you have bad days. *Steven Sidebattom, 14*

EDITOR'S NOTE: Children with dyslexia have a difficulty in learning, reading, writing and language skills. A child's intelligence is normal in all other ways. If the handicap is not recognised and treated, a dyslexic child may never learn to read and may be dismissed as unintelligent. With skilled special teaching children improve and many go on to normal careers.

It's hard to be me, as I am dyslexic, and if you don't no what it is like to be dyslexic, then you are not missing anything. Dyslexia consists of a great deal of problems, mostly reading, writing and spelling, and getting things back to front, so you will probably find that alot of dyslexic children hate school, because they are thout of as thick.

I am hoples at French, so bad that my french teacher asked my parents if I could give it up.

I find my Biolage hard, especially all the long names. When it comes to dictation I get really frustrated because she will dictate a paragraph with a lot of hard spelling words in it and when I ask her how to spell it she tells me to look in my notes and by the time I have found all the spellings she has finished dictating the next sentens (with more hard spelling). So now I just spell them how I think, which is no were ner how they should be spelt.

Another problem is that I speak funny, or prounounce a word wrong, and then I get teased. I used to say low the morn, instead of mow the lawn, or car motor instead of motor car and people thought I had brain damage.

Alot of people say I am not trying, but that is no way true, as I must work at least four times as hard as any other normal person.

About a year ago I would finish my prep at about ten o'clock at night, starting at six o'clock. Because of this, and me being behind at school I became emotionally frustrated.

Before I end this essay I must just say that Dyslexic children are not thick. Alot of people think they are, but they are cirtanaly not!!!

Amanda

When I krt reed peopally fink I have a bag of penuts for a bran and fink i am plient   TrAcy 9 yes old

When I can't read people think I have a bag of peanuts for a brain and think I am blind.

Tracy, 9

About eczema

One day recently the eczema on my arms was quite bad. When I took my jumper off in school some of the girls said unkind things. When I told my mom that night, she suggested I took a "Let's Talk About You" leaflet to show the class. When the girls were nasty again I gave the leaflet to the teacher and she read it out to the class. She also touched my eczema with her hand then put it on her own face to show the class it is not infectious.

Now, instead of saying unkind things they ask me if it is getting better.

Perhaps this story will help other children if they find that their friends do not really understand about eczema.

Nicola Stuart, 8

Lots and lots of children over the world, including myself, have eczema. I will start by talking about the way I feel about having eczema. I feel a lot of frustration when I itch, and feeling sorry for myself makes it worse. Also sometimes I don't itch, but then it's sore! So I'm in a two way trap.
Eczema leads to other problems like diets. I am allergic to wheat, milk, apples, eggs and chicken. It's very hard to avoid eating all those foods. But you can't help breaking your diet once in a while can you? So I just try very hard not to be tempted. It's boring — all those bandages and creams, diets and doctors etc.
But wait. You see you've got to live with it so . . . all you have to do is make the best of it. I mean, try to do nice things and then you won't have to think once about that horrible eczema of yours.

Shelley Shenker, 8

Having eczema is not very nice because you keep on scratching and it hurts, and your clothes sometimes stick to you. And sometimes my legs are so dry I just cannot straighten them. And at night, night always seems worse than daytime. And sometimes I have a bad night's sleep so that means that I am very tired and I do not want to go to school next morning and I nearly always have to go but sometimes I don't. And people at school are always kind to me if they know me, but if they do not know me they are rude to me.
I don't like hot weather because it makes me itch. And when I am not feeling very well at school I always look forward to hometime. I have had eczema since I was five weeks old, but I hope that I will grow out of it one day. Some days I feel very depressed but on the whole it is not too bad.

Tessa Read, 7

Dear helen I have EcSema It makes
Me itch and Some boys at School
thay call Me Flea bag and
Smelly. It makes Me Sad
and I'm on a diet I carnt
have. Some things I like
My hands, feet and knees are
red and crackd and It makes Me
Scatch a SpeShely at night
I wish Some thing could make Me
better

Love Polly

My EcSema

Polly Thorpe, 8

About blindness

People help us blind people too much. They know too little, especially when they cross a street. They just pull and push you, and you don't know when you will reach the pavement on the other side. They walk too fast, that's my opinion. Can't you walk a little slower? You walk much too fast. We must teach them what it's like to be visually handicapped.

Anita Svedin, 12

People should have more thought about leaving bikes, parked cars and prams on pavements. It is very dangerous for a blind person who might bump into them.
Karen Hoffmann, 16

People with normal sight are often unaware of the difficulties partially sighted and blind people experience in their everyday lives. How could they?
I feel that there are a number of things which would help. Firstly, if steps were all edged with white paint (I know that some are) there would be no problem. I think it would be a good idea to have a voice recorded timetable at underground stations. Also in the trains and buses a recording announcing the station or arrival of the vehicle at a stop would help.
Moira Gladwish

I can see a little and I am happy about that. I use the little sight I have as much as I can. I can feel my way. Small things I feel with my fingers and big things I see with my eyes.
Thord Olsson, 14

EDITOR'S NOTE: Be careful when you try to help a blind person in the street. I received many, many complaints from children that people who tried to help often landed up hindering. Remember that on the whole blind people walking along a street wouldn't be there unless they felt that they could cope.
It is obviously quite different if you see a blind person about to fall down a hole, or tread in some dog dirt or encounter some hazard. But it is interesting that I had more requests to be left alone than to be helped. This is because some people who 'help' take the blind person to the wrong bus stop, or take them off their familiar route, or even end up facing the blind person in the wrong direction.
If you do lead a blind person, don't hold their arm — let them hold yours. Walk slightly ahead, slowly, and make sure you follow their instructions about where they want to go. Tell them if you are coming to a kerb or are about to change direction.

Having attended the school for blind children for four years I had a sincere wish to go to an ordinary school. After a lot of problems I had my wish. I was very happy on my first day at the new school. My friends received me well, but I had to be tested. They put their hands in front of me and asked, 'How many fingers are here?' to see how blind I was, but they soon learned that I was totally blind and that they should not place a school-bag in front of me when I was walking down the corridor.

The first year I had to get used to the new school: the noise, the hours of homework and the breaks with a lot of pupils in the schoolyard. It was a little confusing in the beginning but I soon got accustomed to it and I made close friends. Owing to the good education I had had at the school for blind children I was able to take part fully in the activities at the new school. The teachers here are good at supporting me and besides I have a number of aids, which help. My books are written in the braille system (embossed printing) and I write on my Perkins typewriter so I can read my own exercises. When I am going to write an essay I first write a draft on my Perkins, then I record it on my cassette and at last I copy it on my ordinary typewriter so that others are able to read it. I sometimes use my cassette for reading books and articles and in the lessons I may take notes by means of a mini-cassette.

I have a calculating machine. It works like other calculating machines, but it says the numbers when I touch the keys. It is really a great help to me. The newest aid I have got is an Optacon. It is an instrument, the size of a textbook, which makes it possible for me to read an ordinary text. I have a mini-camera in my right hand and I move it over the text in the book. My left forefinger is put on a finger-plate on which the letters from the text come out as small rods. The Optacon is a great invention because it enables blind people to read ordinary books, newspapers and magazines. In my case I am able to read magazines about my hobby viz. electronics.

The aids I have mentioned help every day at school and at home. If I had not got these aids my education would be reduced and my plans for the future could not be carried out. But I have them, so I am hopeful. Aids are one thing, but contact with other people another thing.

John Tidemann, 16

The Braille alphabet: A blind person 'feels' their alphabet through bumps raised on the surface of the paper.

The day I came home

One day, when I was a third-year student at a certain junior high school, I said to myself, "I'll try to go back home all by myself from school". I had been advised to do so by my teacher before. In those days I myself had somewhere in my mind a kind of consciousness that it was about time for me to make a trip back home for myself. But I still felt uneasy about returning home alone, because I had gone out with the help of a half-blind friend of mine and I had had my mother come and take me home before. But nothing good would happen while I was hesitating. I would dare to go home for myself! Finally I made up my mind to do so.

Fortunately I had been trained to walk around the school building alone. So I tried walking to the nearest railroad station accompanied by my teacher. I practised going to the station in the same way, three times in all. Each time I learned lots

Yasunori

of things, such as the way to the station, how and where to get in or off the train. After a few months' practice and preparation, the day for me to go home alone finally came. On the previous evening I called my mother on the phone and said, "Mom, I'm coming back home by myself tomorrow".

"Are you really all right? Take care not to be run over by a car," Mother said in a tone of surprise and anxiety. "It's quite all right", I answered. Mother continued the similar talk anxiously, and every time I answered cheerfully so that she would feel easy. But the fact was that I had no self-confidence. I could not have a good sleep that night.

The next day, when school was over, I got out of the gate of the dormitory with my legs trembling with uneasiness and expectation. On my way to the station I collided with a telegraph pole and a person until at last I got to a crossing, where I did not know which way to go. I asked a man to tell me the way, but he went away without answering me. Just then a middle-aged woman was kind enough to hold a hand of mine and help me to cross the street. My heart was full of pleasure and gratitude then. Thus I could manage to arrive at the station and get in the train.

I was much relieved to feel my train move. But next came into my mind another anxiety. I had to take care not to go beyond my destination. I thought, "If I had good eyesight, I would not have to count the number of stations I passed". I counted the number of them whenever the train

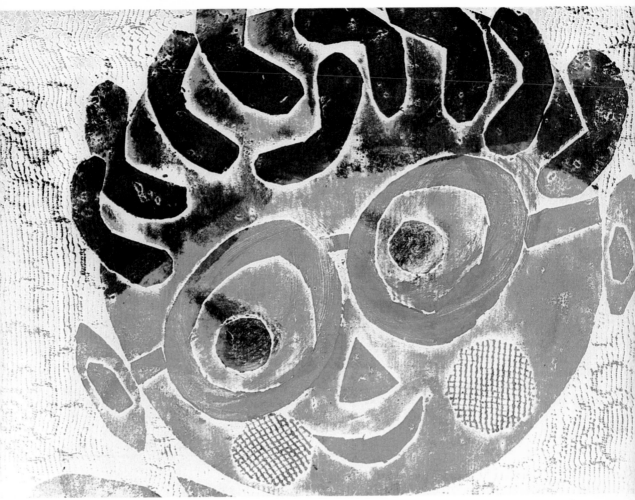

Radim Cagan, 9

stopped at a station. Meanwhile I found myself feeling sleepy. "Oh, no. If I fall asleep, the efforts I have made will come to naught. Hold out!" I said to myself rubbing my eyelids.

In the meantime the train had reached the station where I should get off. "Great! I've arrived at my station", I shouted in spite of myself. As soon as the train stopped, I got out onto the platform quickly. My heart was full of joy. Then I made my way towards my house with light steps, sounding my white stick and feeling the evening sunlight on my back.

"Hello, Mom" I shouted.
"How splendid of you to have been able to come back alone!" said my mother with a smile as she stood at the front door. Then she patted me on the shoulder and showed me into the house, hugging me for joy. That was the most precious experience I had ever had. I felt that the challenge gave me new courage. And I decided to abandon the notion that I cannot do anything because I am totally blind and to go forward with my heart full of joy.

Yasunori Nakagawa

109

About hearing problems

It is not easy to be deaf because it is difficult to communicate. Sometimes hearing people don't understand what I say, so it causes both of us embarrassment. I like people to talk normally but slowly, otherwise I won't be able to follow what they are saying.

I remember one day a few years ago I was waiting for the bus. It was full up but luckily I got in. Then suddenly the people in the bus kept looking at me. I wondered why. After a few minutes I realised that the bus conductor was shouting at me. I felt so embarrased and kept telling myself not to cry. I had no idea why he was shouting at me. Eventually I had to tell him that I was deaf. But he was still the same. He just said something else which I couldn't follow. As soon as possible I got off the bus. I was so relieved, and was still thinking about it all the way home. When I got home I burst out with the story to my mother.

Sometimes it is very difficult for deaf people to pay for tickets at the Underground because they have to say where they are going. Sometimes the people at the ticket office don't understand. The people who are lining up behind the deaf person stare at the deaf person, who feels so small and embarrassed.

It all depends on people's lip movements. Some are very easy; they talk quite openly. But others are so difficult because they just mumble. I love going out with hearing people and I am very happy with them because then I don't feel left out.

Jane Whitaker, 16

Na-Jung Lee

Until I was eleven I tried to talk to people. But sometimes they didn't understand and I got very angry with them. Sometimes it is difficult to talk to new people. Sometimes I don't use my voice. When I was twelve, I learned how to talk with my voice. Sometimes I felt ashamed of myself but my Mum told me if people don't understand what I say, write a note or try again.

When I was young, I never talked to people with my voice and I was always shy to talk. Now, I understand. I must use my voice if I talk. Sometimes people think I am deaf and dumb. *Sharon Tebbutt, 14*

I would like people who can hear to know how to make friends with the deaf because those who can hear believe that the deaf are mentally retarded.

I would like it if when I join children who are playing and I ask them to let me play, they would accept me willingly because usually they think I am mentally retarded and might act awkwardly. *Daniel Garriga, 14*

I envy hearing people. I can't hear the wind blowing or the birds' song. I can hear music but not the words. I can't understand the television conversation. I can hear the sound from an aeroplane if it flies close to the ground, but not far from the ground. I can't hear the prairie birds' drumming. I cannot hear the baby's voice. I would love to hear a baby's voice.

I can't hear the policecar's siren. I can't hear the water flowing slowly. Mostly, I'm happy that I'm not a cripple or blind. I'm happy that I'm deaf. *Crystal Humeston, 15*

EDITOR'S NOTE: When a deaf person is trying to read your lips, be prepared to take the whole conversation more slowly than usual, and don't be embarrassed if you have to repeat things two or three times. Deaf people often have very little opportunity for communication, and the biggest gift you can give is time to listen and to enable them to enjoy the rare pleasure of a simple conversation. Speak only a little louder than normal — shouting never helps. Face the light so that the deaf person can see your lips clearly, and speak slowly. When you get a reply, it may be too loud, too soft, very high pitched or all too often unintelligible!

Can you imagine learning to write without ever seeing your writing? Deaf people can't hear themselves speak so they have no feedback and sometimes don't even know if they have been voicing at all. They also sometimes get the rhythm of a sentence completely wrong. Again, your gift is time. If you can't understand don't make an excuse and dash off. Bother to stay and listen. Bother to communicate. Bother to learn the language of your new deaf friend.

About hearing problems

What frustration! What's the matter with the world! You don't think handicapped children can live normally, but we can. We can talk by writing with a pen and pads. We can communicate with you by clearly lip-reading or sign language. You should talk, not ignore me or leave me alone. We are not mentally retarded, because you think we can't do everything. We can do everything you do. Except use the telephone or hear the TV or radio. You and your friends chat in front of me. What about me? All I want is fair treatment and to have things the same as you. We hope you will learn.

Eleanor Hasko, 14

I like to talk to hearing people but I am very shy with them. Some people are very surprised that I can speak. Some people talk to me but I don't understand and I feel very embarrassed. Some people say the deaf are dumb or mute and I feel hurt. Most people feel sorry for me, but I don't like that because I don't want pity. Most hearing people do not understand sign language. Are you interested in learning sign language?

Alva Kostyshyn

My parents can speak in sign language but my brother can't. I can communicate with my friends but few people are interested in learning sign language. I live in a little town, and don't have many friends.

Bonnie Harding, 18

For twelve and a half years I couldn't talk. I used a speechboard, a typewriter, and my hands to communicate with my family, friends and teachers. Before I learned to spell, it was very hard for them to know what I wanted.

When I was twelve, I saw a machine called a Handi-Voice, which is a precision electronic speech synthesizer for people who can't talk. It has a voice kind of like a robot. It will speak, save, recall or repeat any message. Now I could talk with my family. I called my sister a turkey. She said that the Handi-Voice said that, not me.

A new world has opened up for me since I got the machine. I use it in school and at home. The one thing I really very much **appreciate** is if people give me time to talk. For example, when a teacher asks the class a question, and I know the answer. She or he will see that I'm pushing in the answer in the Handi-Voice. When I'm ready I push a button and it talks for me. Some people, like my family, friends and teachers can make out what the voice is saying. But others can't make out a darn word.   *Jason J. Homyshin, 13*

Lui Tat Shing, 9 ▶

About muscular dystrophy

An Incurable Disease

My incurable disease became apparent when I was four years old. The disease is progressive and often leads to death*. I never expected that it would be so hard for me. My friends, boys and girls, were always faster than me, I was always last. I had been trying to participate in various games. In 1972 I went to the rehabilitation centre in Konstancin. This was my first encounter with disabled people. I remember that I was crying very much when my parents left me there. At that time, I saw for the first time a wheelchair and this was frightening me. On the other hand, I was pleased that I was among people like myself.

It is so hard to go away from parents and from friends. Unfortunately such is fate and it must be taken as it is. Since 1977 I have stayed at the Rehabilitation Centre for Disabled Children at Police. This is a boarding school for craftsman training. I was very pleased when I was accepted here. One boy who was taken with the same disease stayed here, but his condition was much worse. Also, when I was doing my best to be self-sufficient, my friend preferred to ask somebody to help him. Looking at my friend, I was afraid that soon I would also become so disabled. I noticed that my condition was becoming worse. I encountered more difficulties in climbing the stairs, getting up from the bunk during the lesson, etc. I became aware that my illness is progressive. I wonder if this will stop and, if so, when it will stop. I even started to think I would never learn any profession at all.

In 1980 I started becoming more

Marek playing chess with a friend.

114

optimistic. My friend returned after the holidays, but he was very weak, hardly moving on his own. I was very surprised to note that his condition had worsened so much during two months. Therefore, I became more conscious that I must keep training and take every opportunity of rehabilitation. I am frightened whenever I think that shortly I shall have to use a wheelchair.

My happiest day was in 1978: while staying in Konstancin during the vacation, I met a very nice girl. We are still very friendly. I am now in the eighth class and my condition is quite good. I hope that everything will be well. I intend to continue learning and probably I shall try to specialise in Radio and TV repairs. I am very optimistic regarding my future.

Beyond learning, I devote quite a lot of time to scouting and protection of the natural resources. All this makes me very busy and I forget about my disease. All the people around treat me very nicely even though they all are very similar to me. We are enjoying our lives.

Marek Kapusta, 14, Poland

The doctors believe I have a disease called Muscular Dystrophy. Whatever it is, I've got it and have to live with it, which I accept, and will do my utmost to lead my life as normally as I can.

I first went to a special school. I was very happy, but they couldn't really give me the education I required. I am quite lucky in that I am reasonably academically clever. It was decided that I should go full time to an ordinary school in Watford. The first year was hard for both me, the teachers and my fellow pupils. It has all turned out well. I have made many friends, although they were amazed and confused to begin with.

I have been allowed a great opportunity and I must show other people that the idea of handicapped people going into an ordinary school can work. I must pave the way for more children to follow in my tracks.

Really the past is no good to me anymore. It's the future that's my challenge, as it is to all handicapped persons.

I hope I haven't rambled on as I tend to do, but I have just tried to put over that I don't think because a person is physically handicapped they should be treated differently. We can be useful to the human society and I personally am going to. I like being me, it's a challenge!

Marc O'Shaughnessy, 16

EDITOR'S NOTE: Muscular dystrophy is one of the commonest kinds of long term disabling disease. Its effects are a gradual wasting and weakening of the muscles until they can become virtually useless. Children who have got the disease know that they will suffer from it all their life. There is a severe form of muscular dystrophy which leads to early death.

There are other chronic long term diseases like cystic fibrosis and many of the children who contributed to this book have diseases which could affect them all their lives — conditions like epilepsy, asthma and heart trouble.

About mentally handicapped kids

I hate being called a retard because it really hurts. Its so hard trying to make friends with students when they tease me and talk behind my back. Sometimes I feel like being alone. Sometime I wish I didn't have any friends. Sometimes I wish I was different. Sometimes I wish they would think how much there hurting me.

Janice Kreese

I wish I were in another school. Where they could not bug me any more. But really I don't want to move to another school. In my other school people called me wormskinner, ugly and fleebag. Now these here words I do not like.

Corinna Ehrmann

It is very difficult to learn something that you really want to know. Sometimes I am a little slow. My worst thing is trying to know how to measure. I like to be treated nice. I don't like to be treated mean. Why can't I do things well like the other students can do? You can get along with a kid if you don't say anything dum to him.

Martin Hohl

I feel upset being handicapped and outher people make fun of me. They call me names and tease me. When I rode my bike they called me retard. They said I couldn't ride my bike so I told my mom and they didn't do it any more. When you can't do some of the outher stuff that kids do? that's why I don't like being handicapped. You can't do it fast like outher kids and one day thy said I can't learn any thing and I was crieing. That hurt me a lot so I thought I go to another school and learn. I am glad I came here because I learned a lot since I came here. I whish I wasn't like that. That is why I don't like being me. I will be happier if I get better.

Dori Dube

I hate people looking at me sometimes calling me stupid names and swear words. And making ugly faces at me and putting the middle finger up. They're always kicking me in the leg and punching me where it counts and hitting me in the back of the head and sitting on top of me. I have some problems.

Grant Kitchen

Car, truck, train for a ride with Tracy. Yeah friend pussy white — eggbert.

Stephen Brancatisiano, 16

Stephen dictated this entry to his teacher because he can't write. Stephen is able to learn many things but some retarded children can't even learn to talk. Despite this, they still need kindness and love. They may not be able to learn to do a lot of things, but most of them learn to hurt without any effort!

Of course, the children with the very worst handicaps can't speak out for themselves through this book.

Dear Jack,
Thanks for being a good friend. I have never had a good friend that gose places with and found some one that listens and dosn't turn their back on you. I like to work with you. Best part of it is he dosn't turn away when I need him. We do a lot together. Hope it lasts. When I got a job he was very glad about it. He told me what to do he made me feel real good. Because I have a friend that cares a lot for me. Some people make friend this easy. But other people have a hard time makeing friend. Thank for takeing out time to help me.

    Thanks a lot for being a good friend.

                  Mike

              Mike Murphy

This painting by Michel Thommen who is severely mentally handicapped demonstrates great sensitivity to beauty. Other pictures expressed anger and depression. In many ways these were amongst the most emotionally aware of all the pictures we received.

Facing death

These comments were made by boys who know they're dying of a terminal disease:

I would like to be considered as a normal person, but they do not consider normal for us that which is normal for a healthy person. That which is normal for a healthy adolescent, is no longer within our scope.
Death, sexuality, there is only that. We think of other things — of meeting girls just as we are. The problems which that poses are monstrous; you end up feeling abnormal and a little guilty as well. It's annoying that adults begin to gossip as soon as one meets a girl. They think immediately about sexual advancements, etc whereas for me it is completely the opposite. I feel fine with a girl when I chat with her, when we smoke a cigarette together and that's all. Where in fact is the problem? I almost have something to laugh about!

. . . .

There are some things which one just cannot talk about with adults. Death is one of these issues. People prefer to ignore it; they really do deceive themselves over the whole thing. If some of their friends are so ill that they land up in hospital, they end up saying that it really would be better if they died so that they shouldn't suffer too much. It may be hard but . . .
Adults talk about death; about our dying. They even anticipate it! We prefer to wait until it happens! We'll just wait and see, and in the meantime it's not worth worrying about. For the present, we are too busy living, being here and making the best of every moment and then we'll see!
One must dispel this fear of death. The only way to react, when you see the anguish which overtakes adults and the staff, is to laugh and react with a certain cynicism (turning to an adult and saying, for instance, "Good morning, I'm going to spit.") That anguish and fear that they have, what one really wants is for it to just disappear because of what one has said. .

. . . .

Yes, it happens that adults dehumanise us. Grown-ups are afraid that reality is too hard for the young ones to accept and they have a tendency to class us all in the same category.
At the centre certain things are hidden from us. That way, it is easier for adults and they also want to control our lives. Gradually, while we are here, we discover what's hidden from us, and it is that which upsets us. To speak of our death, of sexuality, the adults wear soft gloves or hold meetings and the young ones are excluded from these meetings.
There are discussions with us but they are useless because the adults do not say what they are thinking. They'll say it out of a meeting (they don't say the same things if the younger children don't go to it) They would do better to discuss things with us. They would not be off course any longer. One

wonders if adults sometimes only have meetings simply to have a clear conscience, rather than to understand us better.

. . . .

Morale, that's the main thing. If you don't have it, you go to pieces. And that has repercussions at the physical level, and on the progress of our disease. Yes, the advancement of terminal illness depends a lot on strength of mind. Adults must not only think of our physical well being. That means that primarily one is not treated as an ill person but as a person who wants to be in control, to explain himself — even if it is difficult. Someone who is badly physically disabled, if he has strength of mind, if he can feel himself to be someone, if he has the feeling that he is being given the chance to live, then he is O.K.

. . . .

Left — At Night
Night draws her curtain, time love, leave time.
Remain in our memory of wonder and joy.
Remember the emptiness,
The uselessness of night.
But love I see through night's valley of gloom,
The hillock of death . . .
Entwined a stranger, a murderer of life,
Frosted, frozen face ever facing,
Driven by the power of family withdrawn,
By fields of midnight castles, ogres all hide,
The twisting, the turning,
The fighting of death,
Sigh and refuse God, but life he returns.
Sudden the silence,
Besides death-defiance, or single quest sworn,
They rise and life's released;
The clock ticks again.
I remember the day, the glorious clasp of life,
Hold the day.
Return to our heaven, remembered my love,
Forgotten the blackness of life.

Kim Williams

Kim Williams died of cancer when she was fifteen. She endured a great deal of suffering but was very courageous. Her poems have been published in "The Stone of Life".

My wish for others like me

My Wishes on Behalf of All the Handicapped of This World.
In my room I have a very well-equipped library, which I treat like my treasure. I love reading and my parents get me scientific books, interesting ones and ones of great value.

This library represents for me an enormous window opening onto the whole world, where I can dream and make plans for the near and distant future.

My wish would be that the children of the world have the same opportunities to study, to improve their education and to take part in the cultural amusements, which up to now have only been available to the sound in body.

My second wish would be that humanity pools its financial, material and scientific resources towards medical research to prevent and eradicate the different illnesses which up till now have remorselessly plagued people throughout the world.

Jan Boksansky

Three Wishes

My first wish is that every child, every physically handicapped person should be able to take part in cultural things — visit theatres, cinemas, exhibitions and libraries without difficulty. And to visit supermarkets and above all work, because every handicapped person is very keen to be useful to human society.

I know only too well from my own experience how important it is to a handicapped person to be able to be useful to his neighbour and to be capable of taking care of himself without asking for help from anyone. Helping is a tremendously pleasant sensation.

It is also very important for us to be understood and liked by our friends and neighbours, and not only by one person. All the well-intentioned people should themselves consider that they have no guarantee that they will stay healthy their whole lives. Whether their eventual suffering is visible or not — it is sometimes quite enough to understand that the handicapped have a right to fulfil their own lives. That is my second wish.

The third, and most important wish, is that all the children of the world should live in peace, without fear and worry and without experiencing famine. Only then can all the good will, all the efforts expended daily for the handicapped, be worthwhile and important.

This, my final wish, is the most important without doubt. For, without peace, and without security my previous desires would make no sense at all.

Marie Procházková

120

All the children of the world, I love you. And whether you are blind or handicapped, I love you all, absolutely everyone.

Sophie Beaulieu, 7

My three wishes for all the handicapped children of the world are independence and acceptance. I wish that all the disabled children of the world may stop thinking "Why me?" and just accept that they have been chosen to lead a very different kind of life and I wish them all happiness in whatever they do and wherever they may be.   *Heather Jones*

I shall set up a factory when I am grown up, a furniture factory. I will employ only deaf workers, and it will be first factory of its kind in Pakistan.

Bahadur Jamil

Lai Hung Leung

Dear God
I am a boy from Korea, on the eastern side
of the Earth.
In all countries of the world,
In every land,
Please make for us a world
Without war, without hunger,
And without worry.

Dear God
That we may overcome the pain of
disability,
Give us a heaven-like world where
Peace and
Love and
Contentment
Bloom like flowers.

Keum Shik No

If I were cured

Tracey

"Tracey, what would you do if for one magic week you could walk?"
"I'd hoover the whole house for me Mom. And dust and things. I'd love to do the hoovering and things for her."

Tracey Bill, 11

I like to read books very much. People call me "a bookworm" I try to understand the heroine and I think what I would have done in her place. I imagine myself to be healthy, walking to school like others, playing with other children. I think what it would be like if I did not have to take care about every step. Sometimes I dream that I am healthy and that together with my sister or brother I go to a cinema or a dancing party.

Danuta Gieraltowska, 16

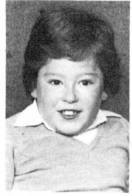

Stephen

"What would you do if for one magic week you could walk?"
"I wouldn't go to sleep. I'd stand. I wouldn't want to do anything else really. Just stand without this silly old wheelchair. Just stand all the time."

Stephen Rolt, 11

If I wasn't handicapped I would be able to run, play games and ride a horse. I could dance and climb and go up the slide and do gymnastics, be a majorette and thump my little brother!

Kristina Righart

Me, I'd like to be normal. Like that I'd go to the toilet all by myself.
Christophe Denis, 12

If I wasn't handicapped I could go on school trips to different countries. And I could play football. And I could go on a paper round and if I wasn't handicapped I couldn't get into a fairground free. And I could join the Air Force driving a helicopter or be a Wing Commander, and I could be a Policeman, or a Detective or a Train Driver driving the Intercity 125 or a Water Man. *Robert Malcolm Senthouses, 10*

If I were cured I would ride my bike and I would run, I'd fool about, I'd play ball, I'd go to see my Dad and Mum in the garden all by myself.
Laurence Hypeau, 10

122

Alexandra Kosobucha

Jana Polaskova

A special thank you

To My Grandparents

Thank you both for what you've done
You have pulled me through:
We have been through thick, through thin
Even though we ceaselessly cry
Always asking questions. Why?
Always doubting, always fighting
Coming through, however frightening.

Timothy Clark, 13

I thank you Dr. James G. Manson for saving my life and much deeper, for your donation of free service.

Dr. Manson, I want you to know that you have brought my whole life to a new stage, relieved me from the pain I've suffered since childhood. I feel I am a new person. You changed my whole life to a full functioning individual.

Several things that I could not do before, I am now able to do, e.g. I can walk a hundred blocks in less than thirty minutes. My future looks great. Finally, I thank you for your great empathy, love and the interest you show in me. Your excellent work on my knee has given a new leg for life. Keep up good work. I promise to remain your friend forever.   *Saul Mkabi*

My family (including my fourteen year old brother, David) have all been marvellous, helping me along the path of life. There have been some stones in that path, but together we flattened them and carried on as before. Some of these have been my hospital visits, but I can honestly say that there was *always* someone there to cheer me up. I have been fortunate in not having to have many operations, but I have had quite a few. Let's just say I could count them on two hands, for fear of being thought boastful! Many of those were to help me walk, and I can console the surgeons by saying that although I don't walk much, I do walk a little and that it was not a waste of time.

Helen Bryant, 12

All the staff at Fountaindale where I go, are wonderful people. Some of them I have known for nine years and others only a few months. Whoever I have gone to, in all of my nine years at school, has always been ready to help or advise me. I think that almost any child, no matter how simple or bad their disability is, will tell you that somewhere in their lives people were always ready to help them.

We do not often wallow in self pity, but when we are feeling a bit depressed, you can be absolutely sure that there will be someone there to comfort us. THANK YOU.

Erica Lockhart, 13

My thanks go to all the schools and organizations who helped with this book. They include:

CADIS, Buenos Aires, **Argentina**.
Institute for Speech and Hearing, **Argentina**.
Allambie School & Treatment Centre, The Spastic Centre of New South Wales, Allambie Heights, **Australia**.
Bellhaven School for Intellectually Handicapped Children, Young, New South Wales, **Australia**.
Spastic Children's Society of Victoria, South Yarra, **Australia**.
Sydenham/Bankstown Day School, Sub-Normal Children's Welfare Association, Sydney, **Australia**.
Lower Secondary State School, Bouwvarniknerhed, Dilsen, Hasselt, **Belgium**.
State School for the Handicapped, Gent, **Belgium**.
Woudlucht, Heverlee, Louvain, **Belgium**.
Acadiaville School, West Arichat, Richmond County, Nova Scotia, **Canada**.
AQETA, Bell Canada & Regional Education Commission for Chambly, Quebec, **Canada**.
Arcadia Consolidated School, Yarmouth County, Nova Scotia, **Canada**.
Cerebral Palsy School, c/o Stonepark Junior High School, Charlottetown, Prince Edward Island, **Canada**.
Chaplin Elementary School, Saskatchewan, **Canada**.
Dartmouth Public Schools, Nova Scotia, **Canada**.
Glenrose School Hospital, Edmonton, Alberta, **Canada**.
Horizon School for the Mentally Handicapped, Olds, Alberta, **Canada**.
Lindsay Place High School, Pointe Claire, Quebec, **Canada**.
Lord Roberts Community School, Winnipeg, Manitoba, **Canada**.
Macdonald High School, Lakeshore School Board, Beaconsfield, Quebec, **Canada**.
Manitoba School for the Deaf, Winnipeg, Manitoba, **Canada**.
Musquodoboit Rural High School, Halifax, Nova Scotia, **Canada**.
Sir Frederick Fraser School, Halifax, Nova Scotia, **Canada**.
Sr. Wm. Osler Vocational School, Orthopaedic Class "The Wheelers", Agincourt, Ontario, **Canada**.
Virginia Waters School, St. John's, Newfoundland, **Canada**.
Centre for Cerebral Palsy, Zeleznice, **Czechoslovakia**.
Federal National Council for the Disabled, Prague, **Czechoslovakia**.
Institute for the Disabled, Brně-Králově, Poli, **Czechoslovakia**.
Primary School for Children with Poor Eyesight, Opava, **Czechoslovakia**.
School for the Deaf, Hořičkach, **Czechoslovakia**.
School for the Deaf, Ivančicích, Brno, **Czechoslovakia**.
Special School for Physically Handicapped Children, Dr. Jedlicka Institute, Prague, **Czechoslovakia**.
Zakladni Skola, Pod Lipami, **Czechoslovakia**.
Council for Special Education, Copenhagen, **Denmark**.
Nordre Skole, Viborg, **Denmark**.
School for the Deaf, Kuopio, **Finland**.
School for Imparied Hearing, Jyväskylä, **Finland**.
Centre for Physically Handicapped Children, Paris, **France**.
CNFLRH, Paris, **France**.
National Association for the Rehabilitation of the Handicapped, Paris, **France**.
Department of Special Education, Deurne, **Holland**.
John F. Kennedy Centre, Hong Kong Red Cross, **Hong Kong**.
Victoria Park School for the Deaf, Causeway Bay, **Hong Kong**.
Bjarkarasi School for the Handicapped, Reykjavik, **Iceland**.
Hope Valley Experimental Special Education Unit, Mona Rehabilitation Centre, Kingston, **Jamaica**.
Special Schools of Japan, Tokyo, **Japan**.
Joytown Special School for Physically Handicapped Children, Thika, **Kenya**.
Attached Primary School, Children's Rehabilitation Centre, Yonsei University Medical Centre, Seoul, **Republic of Korea**.
Daegu Bogun School for the Crippled, **Republic of Korea**.
National School for the Deaf, Seoul, **Republic of Korea**.
Seoul Aie Whoa School, Seoul, **Republic of Korea**.
Carlson School, Auckland, **New Zealand**.
Laura Fergusson Home for the Disabled, Green Lane, Auckland, **New Zealand**.
Long Bay College, Auckland, **New Zealand**.
Matariki Physically Handicapped Unit, Macandrew Intermediate School, Dunedin, **New Zealand**.
Mt. Roskill Grammar Physically Handicapped Unit, Auckland, **New Zealand**.
New Zealand Crippled Children Society (Auckland, Marlborough, Nelson, South Canterbury and Southland Branches), **New Zealand**.

126

Physically Handicapped Unit, Papatoetoe South School, Auckland, **New Zealand**.
Royal New Zealand Foundation for the Blind, Homai College, Manurewa, **New Zealand**.
School for the Physically Disabled, Christchurch, **New Zealand**.
Wellington Crippled Children Society, Johnsonville, **New Zealand**.
Wilson Home School, Takapuna, Auckland, **New Zealand**.
Oluyole Cheshire Home for the Physically Handicapped, Ibadan, **Nigeria**.
Pacelli School for Blind Children, Lagos, **Nigeria**.
School for the Deaf, Ibadan, **Nigeria**.
School for the Deaf and the Blind, Ilorin, Kwara State, **Nigeria**.
Linde School for the Handicapped, Tonsberg, **Norway**.
Deaf and Dumb High School for Boys, Lahore, **Pakistan**.
Centre for Special Education (Arequipa, Lima and Piura branches), **Peru**.
Educational Centre for Crippled Children, Busko Resort, **Poland**.
Educational Centre for the Deaf, Warsaw, **Poland**.
Kuratorium Oswiaty i Wychowania, Lublin, **Poland**.
Maria Grzegorzewska Centre of Schooling and Education for Crippled Children, Police, **Poland**.
Panstwowy Zaklad Wychowawczy, Slawno, **Poland**.
Urzad Wojewodzki, Lublin, **Poland**.
National Secretariat for the Disabled, Lisbon, **Portugal**.
Special School for the Blind and Partially Sighted, Solna, **Sweden**.
Central Council for Schools and Institutions, Berne, **Switzerland**.
Day School for Cerebral Palsy, Zurich, **Switzerland**.
School for the Deaf and Dumb, St. Gallen, **Switzerland**.
Sonnenhof Home for the Handicapped, Arlesheim, **Switzerland**.
Council on Social Welfare of Thailand, Bangkok, **Thailand**.
Association for Spina Bifida and Hydrocephalus (Coney Hill School, Kent, and Thomas Parker School, Telford), **United Kingdom**.
British Epilepsy Association, Wokingham, Berkshire, **United Kingdom**.
Corseford School for Spastics, Kilbarchan, Renfrewshire, **United Kingdom**.
Dr. Barnardo's (Ian Tetley Memorial and Princess Margaret Schools), **United Kingdom**.
Dyslexia Institute, Staines, Middlesex, **United Kingdom**.
Fountaindale School, Mansfield, Nottinghamshire, **United Kingdom**.
Foxdenton School, Chadderton, Oldham, Lancashire, **United Kingdom**.
Franklin Delano Roosevelt School, London, **United Kingdom**.
Garvel Deaf Centre, Greenock, Strathclyde, **United Kingdom**.
Hangers Wood School, South Oxhey, Hertfordshire, **United Kingdom**.
John Aird School for Blind and Partially Sighted Children, London, **United Kingdom**.
John Chilton School, Northolt, Middlesex, **United Kingdom**.
Kingsley School, Kettering, **United Kingdom**.
Lord Mayor Treloar College, Lower School, Froyle, Hampshire, **United Kingdom**.
Murrayfield School for Spastics, Edinburgh, **United Kingdom**.
National Eczema Society, Norwich, Norfolk, **United Kingdom**.
Oak Lodge School for the Deaf, London, **United Kingdom**.
PHAB (Fairfax, Huddersfield and Oswestry Clubs), **United Kingdom**.
Queen Mary's Hospital School, Carshalton, Surrey, **United Kingdom**.
Sandall Wood School, Doncaster, **United Kingdom**.
Spinal Injuries Association, London, **United Kingdom**.
Sybil Elgar School, The National Society for Autistic Children, London, **United Kingdom**.
Ysgol Gogarth, Llandudno, Gwynedd, **United Kingdom**.
Sahuaro High School, Tucson, Arizona, **USA**.
John Milton Society for the Blind, New York, NY, **USA**.
Jamie Schuman Center, River Vale, NJ, **USA**.
Easter Seal Society of Central Pennsylvania, Bloomsburg PA, **USA**.

We gratefully acknowledge permission to include the following material:
"Mothers" from *Damn-Burst of Dreams*, published by Weidenfeld and Nicolson; 'Left — at Night' from *The Stone of Life* by Kim Williams, published by Franklin Watts; extracts from an article by Helen Franks, published in *Good Housekeeping*; and an extract from *Exchange* no. 3 Autumn 1976, published by the National Eczema Society.

Other interesting books from Friendship Press

Roots and Wings
Elaine Ward
This collection of children's stories looks at the kind of uprootedness children experience in their daily living — through divorce, illness, moving, separation from parents and loved ones. Life-like drawings of children of various racial and ethnic origins and discussion questions enhance the book. (Grades 1-6). $3.95   00130-9.

Stories from Three Islands
Haiti, Jamaica, Puerto Rico
Ruth Montgomery and Edna McGuire
Songs, dances, stories, games — all the different ways children can express themselves, and most of all show joy — the Haitian, Jamaican and Puerto Rican children's way. Includes drawings by and photos of children of the Caribbean and teacher's guidance. $3.25   00064-7.

Clues to Creativity
Vol. I, II, III
M. Franklin and Maryann J. Dotts
A three-volume series on learning and the creative arts. Designed for busy teachers, the more than 100 activities are listed alphabetically from Acting Out/Drama, Banners and Beads to Video-tape, Weaving, Wire sculpture and Writing. Class-tested, they will enliven your teaching and secure class participation. Each $4.95   00015-9; 00041-8; 00042-6.

Children's Games from Many Lands
Edited by Nina Millen
A treasury of some 258 games from Asia, Africa and Latin America as well as Europe and North America. Standard work for every church and library. $5.95   45011-1

Children's Festivals from Many Lands
Nina Millen
Religious and folk festivals from Africa, Asia, Europe, the Americas and the Pacific Islands, with suggestions for use. $4.95   44501-0.

The Runaway Heart
Norma E. Koenig
This collection of short stories for children offers five well-told lessons on the theme of American pluralism. Each story presents a familiar situation containing questions of identity and of America's social diversity, and each refers to basic biblical messages. Includes poetry, "work-space" for reader's responses. $4.95   00112-0.

FREE catalogs available on request. Books may be ordered through your denominational bookstore or from the Friendship Press Distribution Office, P.O. Box 37844, Cincinnati, Ohio 45237. Please add 10% for postage and handling.